# VENTURE INTO HEALING

VENTURE INTO HEALING

# VENTURE INTO HEALING

**F. Roy Jeremiah**

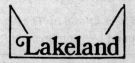

LAKELAND
BLUNDELL HOUSE
GOODWOOD ROAD
LONDON SE14 6BL


© F. Roy Jeremiah 1972

ISBN 0 551 00317 0

*Printed in Great Britain by The Anchor Press Ltd, and bound by Wm. Brendon & Son Ltd, both of Tiptree, Essex*

# CONTENTS

All the incidents in this book took place exactly as described, but in order to respect confidences, names of people and places have sometimes been disguised.

# PREFACE

It has been said that no book should be written without a purpose. As one looks back to the time when Jesus of Nazareth walked this earth, there was a specific occasion when He claimed to be the Son of God. On hearing this the Jews sought to stone Him for blasphemy, but were checked when He said : 'If I do not the works of my Father, believe me not. But if I do, though ye believe not me, believe the works; that ye may know, and believe, that the Father is in me, and I in Him.' In every generation actions speak louder than words. The works of healing and deliverance recorded here were all done in the power of the Holy Spirit by the same Jesus, using human channels whose authority rests only in His name.

At a time when the faith of many Christians is being sorely tried, when there are those even within the Church who add to their confusion by having so analysed the Scriptures as to seemingly paralyse them, it is hoped this simple book will encourage its readers to hold fast to the truth of God's Word. Moreover, each story bespeaks the Living Jesus! He is revealed in His works of supernatural power and compassion in our present generation, notwithstanding the imperfections and failings of those human channels He chooses to use for His purposes of love. Jesus once said : 'He that believeth on me, the works that I do shall he do also . . .' Part of the prayerful purpose of this book is to underline that truth, and at the same time add glory to his name, for He also said: 'Without me you can do nothing.'

F.R.J.

# 1 VENTURE INTO HEALING

The last day of August was sailing day. Lucy and I had looked forward to it with mixed feelings. Now it had dawned. We had made our farewells to our daughters whom we were not to see for well over two years. The house we had liked so much was no longer our home. It stood silent and empty after all the toil of packing up and clearing out. There was a mound of flaky grey ashes at the bottom of the garden which to me at least testified a complete break with the past. They were all that was left of years and years of typed sermons I had sweated and prayed over, preached and kept until now . . . I would never dip into them again, for they were a burnt-offering as unto the Lord who now wished me to preach and practise divine healing. This would be a challenge in itself, for I had never preached one sermon on that subject. However, we believed that where the will of God was sending us, the grace of God would both enable and keep us. Our call was to South Africa. Our venture of faith was to lead us into the healing ministry of the Church of Jesus Christ. He alone knew what lay ahead of us.

As we embarked on the newest ship of the Union Castle Line, the *Transvaal Castle*, the sun shone from cloudless blue skies at Southampton; but we were un-usually quiet, not sharing our thoughts. There had been excitement at the prospect of a voyage into the unknown, neither of us having been to South Africa, but there is always a sadness when leaving one's homeland and friends.

Having sold much of our home we had been rash enough to book a good cabin, not least because in a few days we should celebrate our Silver Wedding. Finding the cabin was a little difficult, but getting into it even more so. There were flowers everywhere: sheaves, bouquets, potted plants, bowls and vases filled with colourful beauty. I felt there was a mistake somewhere—surely this must be for some celebrity, a film star? I said as much to Lucy, who promptly read some of the cards attached . . . no, they were ours, all from well-wishers. We were very touched, knowing that behind their tokens of love were also their prayers for God's blessing upon us.

We made our way to the dining saloon, only to find it very full. It seemed everyone but us had friends or relatives to share a farewell luncheon with; we were not due to sail till 4 p.m. Before we had time to finish our meal we were startled to hear over the intercom a request for us to go to the reception desk. There we found to our great joy two stalwarts from the London staff of the Mission to Lepers; I had worked for that society for the past eight and a half years. As a surprise they had come all that way just to 'wave us off'. All our sadness disappeared!

They had a load of parcels with them—and more flowers! I could only surmise they feared we might starve on the ship. Biscuits, fruit, chocolates, sweets, cakes, fudge . . . the home-made fudge being doled out weeks later to African girls a piece at a time; their eyes rolling with delight at the sweetness of something new.

At the second bell the last of the visitors left, and soon the gangways were raised. On the quay our friends mingled with many others. The ship's band played lively tunes on deck, passengers crowded to the side and threw out myriads of coloured streamers; our ship slipped her moorings and we moved slowly away, at which point the sirens of other ships at berth gave us a shrill 'Bon Voyage', and as our liner moved majestically forward her siren warned other craft to make way. It was a time of emotion which brought a lump to many a throat, and tears to the eyes. Our voyage had begun.

That night, our first at sea, Lucy and I settled in our comfortable beds on either side of the cabin. Most of the flowers had been placed where many people could enjoy them round the ship—or we wouldn't have had room to turn. Convinced that when the Lord gave Lucy a word some weeks before: 'I will make a way in the sea and a path in the mighty waters,' this was His promise to give us a smooth passage, she soon lost any fears. We sailed for a fortnight in calm seas.

Just before switching off my bed light I took my Bible and asked the Lord to give us a word. Opening anywhere I looked at these words: 'Wherefore seeing we also are compassed about with so great a cloud of witnesses, let us lay aside every weight, and the sin which doth so easily beset us, and let us run with patience the race that is set before us, looking unto Jesus the author and finisher of our faith . . .' What could be better? In spite of the strangeness of our surroundings and the gentle swell of the sea, we were soon asleep.

Weeks later we were driven through the streets of Durban, a fine city, and along the beautiful coast to the north. Our destination was a private hospital registered under the Province of Natal, some fifty miles away. This was the Healing Home where we were to spend the next two years in ministry. Everything we saw was a fascination to us, and overhead the African sun shone down from blue skies.

As we motored the last few miles there came a change. Threatening storm-clouds followed us and overtook us, the sun was lost behind them, the temperature fell suddenly. Now, for the first time, we were hearing about the Home and the kind of patients there, of the problems

—or some of them! I gathered that sometimes we might find an alcoholic or two on our hands. In my childhood I had been terrified of drunken men, and that deep-seated fear had never quite left me. True, I had never wanted alcohol for that reason! I learnt later that Lucy too had felt chilled, not just because of a drop in the temperature either. After all, we were about to begin a new work . . . a work which I now know the enemy hates, for it reveals the Living Jesus. Already, the enemy was suggesting doubts to us, then fears . . . but now the car went through the great iron gates behind which impossible things were to happen during our stay there. Things good, and bad, for life is ever a mixture. It is of the good that this book seeks to tell, or a little of it, to add glory to Jesus.

As we reached our rooms the sub-tropical storm broke. Vivid lightning crackled, heavy thunder rolled and echoed for miles it seemed, and torrential rain fell. It passed, as storms do. Next day the sun shone. The Board appointed me Hospital Warden.

## 2 HANNAH

Hannah sat waiting for the Holy Communion service to begin. It was her first visit to this Home of Healing, and she had not been inside the chapel before. She knew it was Anglican, but the fact that she was non-conformist didn't worry her, for all were welcome here. The Prayer Book index had enabled her to find the right page, but she was not conversant with it. The other thing was that Anglicans did more kneeling and uprising than they did in her own church; however, she decided to watch the others and follow suit. She didn't wish to be conspicuous, nor to make a fool of herself.

Looking in front of her she liked what she saw. The altar linen was spotless and well ironed. Flowers in two brass vases were well arranged. She approved of the cleanliness and simplicity. She always kept herself clean and fresh, choosing neat rather than fussy dress. Though approaching three score years she was attractive, and there was a kindly warmth about her that made her likeable.

Above the altar there was a porcelain figure of Christ. She studied it, and decided someone had chosen it with care. Steady flames from the lighted candles enhanced the beauty of the face, revealing both its strength and compassion. Many, in deep need like herself, Hannah thought, must have sat in this chapel and gazed at that Face. How many, she wondered, were healed?

Turning her head she was able to see through one of the long open windows, all of which were set in the south wall. Outside nothing stirred, and remembering it was only eight o'clock she surmised most people would be having an extra lie-in because it was Sunday morning. The immediate view of jacaranda trees, a lawn, and a few rondavels bathed in warm sunshine, was just a sample of the loveliness of Natal. The stillness outside and the quiet of the chapel were such a contrast to the noisy city she was accustomed to that she must surely find some healing by just being here. She had come for three weeks. She was glad she had come. There was peace all around her; but within she was aware there was none. The celebrant began the service. She picked up her open prayer book to follow him, but suddenly he seemed to have gone off at a tangent; she turned several pages, and then gave up, deciding the mysteries of the Book of Common Prayer were only for the initiated. Worship in her own church was made much easier.

During the sermon, try as she would to listen, thoughts of all kinds kept floating up from her subconscious mind. Her husband had been good to let her come, and she hoped he'd manage all right without her. This afternoon would be a good time to send him some impressions of this Home where the Church's ministry of Divine Healing had been practised for nearly twenty years. She must tell him too about her journey here last Friday. How weary she had felt after three hundred miles in that train; though she'd expected that, since it was early January, and midsummer is always so hot anyway. It was nice to chat with the Warden and his wife over a welcome cup of tea. She had made her usual apology, of course: 'Excuse me shaking hands with my left hand, but I can't do it with my right. Three years ago I broke my little finger, and after going to hospital the surgeon said he had done what he could but it would never bend again. I always feel self-conscious about it because it sticks out so—even holding a cup of tea, and strangers must think

I'm pointing at them . . . worst of all, I can never wear a glove on that hand.'

Thinking it over now, Hannah decided her first introduction went well, though the finger was the least of her troubles. Nowadays, though on a strict diet, she often had pains across her chest, and whatever she ate seemed to leave a nasty sour taste in her mouth. She had slipped her x-ray pictures in her suitcase just to show she really had an ulcer; and, of course, she would mention her hiatus hernia at the same time. That really was a nuisance because she loved gardening. Her doctor, a Jew, had said he would operate for the ulcer—unless a miracle of healing took place here. It was nice of him to encourage her to come.

The voice of the preacher cut in upon her reverie. What was he saying? That sooner or later the mind can throw upon our bodies ills of various kinds. She'd never thought of that before, but dwelling on it for a moment she recalled a text: 'As a man thinketh in his heart, so is he'. If that was so, then perhaps her first marriage could account for her ulcer. She hadn't realised until too late that she had married an alcoholic, and only those who do can know what it is like to live with one; she deliberately shut her mind to the memories that often haunted her. Maybe she would tell the Warden a little about that, and she would tell him she had married again.

A hymn she loved followed the sermon, and from that point something seemed to stir within her. Kneeling, she looked again at the figure of Christ on its pedestal, and as she looked fleeting thoughts passed quickly like pictures before her mind's eye. She was not one given to imagination or impulse, but somehow the figure seemed to be looking directly at her, reminding her of things she had done and said, which now made her feel uncomfortable. She loved Jesus, and one of the things she told the Warden was her sense of shame at never being able to pray extemporarily at the prayer meetings in her church. But there were other things now coming up to the surface, things which perhaps her normally bright manner covered up; things like unforgiveness, bitterness, and resentments. To herself she rarely admitted them. Yet He knew they were there, and suddenly she saw them for what they were, saw them as He saw them. She felt unworthy. She did not want those sins; but then, who did? No one, she admitted, ever wanted anyone else's sins, neither your friends nor your enemies. There was only one who dealt with those, Jesus only.

The celebrant turned to face the congregation, and in so doing drew her attention. As she listened to his words they seemed expressly for her. The Invitation in the prayer book she had never heard before: 'Ye that do truly and earnestly repent you of your sins, and are in love and charity with your neighbours, and intend to lead a new life . . . Draw near with faith, and take this Holy Sacrament to your comfort; and make your humble confession to Almighty God . . .'

She could not join in the Confession as she had lost her place in the book, but He knew her heart, which was all that mattered. She whispered her own confession, and heard the priestly Absolution. Then came the well-known words of Jesus: 'Come unto me, all that travail and are heavy laden, and I will refresh you.'

Tears welled up in Hannah's eyes; the grace of penitence overwhelmed her. She wanted to come to Him, to come to His table, but she wrongly supposed she would be turned away since she was not a confirmed member of the Anglican Church. Her heart cried out: 'Lord, I do want to come to your table, but I cannot . . . but I know you will not turn me away.' As the communicants went forward she remained kneeling in her place, and, indeed, until most had left the chapel after the Blessing.

Making her way slowly through the bright sunshine back to her room, she felt strangely at peace with her beautiful surroundings. Yes, she thought, I am glad I came. What she did not know, of course, was that her healing had already begun.

．　　．　　．

At the time Hannah came to the Home, my wife and I were just settling down among a new people to a new work, and, as far as we were concerned, in a new country. That we had been called of God to a healing ministry in South Africa still seemed almost unbelievable, but here we were because we took Him at His word. One thing was certain; we knew we could never heal anyone, and although my wife, Lucy, had read much about divine healing and was keenly interested, I was not. I had a simple faith and believed Jesus sometimes did miracles of healing; realised, too, that miracles often happen in hospitals where doctors, nurses, and other workers give of their best to heal patients; but I knew nothing of their work in preparation for which they had studied for years. Added to that was the fact that I knew almost nothing of the workings of a human body, or brain for that matter, and had no psychiatric training. What then had I to offer?

For seven years I had been a chaplain to mentally and emotionally disturbed people in a small hospital, but this only required a weekly visit as a spiritual worker. It is probable that in those years I gained some knowledge that stood me in good stead when I came into the healing ministry. Other than that, one can hardly be a parish priest for nineteen years, as I had been, meeting all types of people and often trying to help them in times of sickness and stress, without learning much of human nature. I knew how God had also dealt with my own rebellious nature, and when one is honest with oneself one is more likely to be able to understand one's fellows. Yet, could any or all of these equip one for such a ministry? Hardly.

The day on which my call to this work came was the day in which God not only made a promise to give me a blessing, but proved that where He guides, He provides. The call came in the morning, and in the afternoon Jesus baptised me in the Holy Spirit. By the next day I was not only able to speak freely in an unknown tongue, I was also assured that Acts 1:8, 'But ye shall receive power, after that the Holy Ghost is come upon you', was now by His grace put into effect. Time soon proved this, and He has truly blessed our witness both abroad and at home. Every healing and deliverance brings glory to Him. We have had the privilege of playing our part, often with others, and sometimes at considerable cost, as channels of His healing love; we have had the joy, too, of seeing results. What you read in this book is true, and would never have been written but for His direction; therefore He will bless what He calls into being. Nevertheless, as I recall and record these miracles of His redeeming love and healing power, I am conscious of His Word: 'I am the Lord; that is My Name; and My glory will I not give to another' (Isaiah 42:8).

. . .

It was on 13th January, 1963 that Hannah received spiritual blessing at the Communion service, but at the later morning service she came with others and knelt at the altar rail for the laying on of hands with prayer. Seeing Hannah before me I hesitated. I knew only what she had said on her arrival, but forgot she had a finger that wouldn't bend, and knew nothing of her other needs. She was here for a holiday, so I prayed that while she was here she would receive that wholeness which only Jesus can give, and, recalling her fear of praying aloud in company, I asked that she might return to her church as a bold witness to others of the healing Christ, and specifically asked that her fears about extempore prayer would be taken away. We had no personal contact for the next two days.

After breakfast on Tuesday she approached me in the dining room allotted to visitors. When I asked how she was, she answered somewhat miserably, 'I'm not at all well,' and added crossly, 'you know very well I told you I have arthritis.' If she had, I had forgotten, and putting on what I hoped was a sympathetic look, I expressed my regret. It didn't seem to work, for at this juncture she astonished me by saying accusingly, 'I feel terrible, much worse than when I came, and what's more, it's all your fault.'

'Mine?' I enquired. 'Why, what have I done?'

This time she seemed astonished: 'You surely remember what you did on Sunday, when you placed your hands on my head and prayed?'

I admitted that, but felt I was a bit lost in our conversation.

Leaning against the table she queried, 'Didn't you feel anything?'

'No,' I replied, 'did you?'

Back came the answer with some force. 'Of course I did! It was as if some dreadful electric shock went right down from my head to the bottom of my back; I was in such pain I could hardly get to my feet and walk back to my place, and ever since then it has been agonising.'

'Well,' I answered, 'I'm sorry about that; I didn't feel a thing myself, but you ought to cheer up, not complain,' I told her, 'for I believe you are having a healing.'

'A healing!' she echoed, as if doubting my sanity. 'But I feel worse!'

Smiling, and somehow elated, I explained how only the night before I had been reading a book on divine healing, and the author had stated that sometimes people feel more pain after the laying on of hands, in cases, for example, like arthritis. Many decide there is nothing at all in this so-called divine healing, and shed any faith they might have had because they feel worse, whereas if only they had kept their faith and claimed their healing on God's promise, in a few days they would have been free from pain and, in fact, healed.

'Hannah,' I said, 'just you start praising God and thanking Him for your healing, no matter what your feelings are, for I believe you are being healed.'

Her face brightened: 'All right,' she promised. 'I will.'

Next morning, before I had time to say grace at breakfast, she was beside my table: 'I'm sure you're right,' she said, 'for all my pain has gone. I feel so different this morning, I think I must have had a healing.' Her blue eyes sparkled. Then, as if suddenly remembering, she lifted her right hand and waggled her little finger under my nose: 'See!' she cried triumphantly. It was the finger that would not bend.

'When did that happen?' I asked.

A very feminine disarming smile spread over her face: 'Oh, that happened at the altar when you ministered to me with the laying on of hands.'

'Really!' I said. 'If that isn't just like a woman! You moaned about your back, but never said your finger had started to bend after being stiff for three years!'

We laughed together, for joy is infectious. Moreover, it was the first time I knew without a shadow of doubt that the Lord had really used me as a channel of healing in this way.

'Hannah,' I remarked, 'you must have had something wrong with your back, since you felt the pain went there.'

'Never,' she laughed, 'never had a thing wrong with it in the whole of my life.'

I was new to this work, of course, but I was puzzled, and as she left me I called after her, 'The Holy Spirit never makes a mistake.'

On Friday morning my co-Warden took Matins, and I stayed at our house just a few hundred yards from the Healing Home itself. After breakfast Hannah burst upon me as I sat typing at a table on the stoep. I was surprised to see her, and, rising to my feet, said as much.

'I just had to come,' she cried excitedly, 'it's my foot, my foot!'

Nothing registered in my head; maybe it was still a little early in the day for memory to be at work. 'Your foot?' I said with a touch of suspicion. 'Now don't tell me you have anything wrong with your foot!'

'Didn't you know I had an accident six years ago?'

I shook my head, wondering what was coming next.

It came in a rush: 'I thought you knew. Well, I fell down a flight of steps—wooden ones leading on to a beach. I grabbed at the handrail but missed every now and again, and finally landed on the soft sand. I turned over on my foot and broke it badly. They never set it very well, and though a young pastor prayed over it and it improved somewhat, I've had pain in that foot every day for six years. My husband massages it with a little olive oil every night; he's very good.'

Was there anything this woman hadn't had? I asked myself; but she was unaware of my thought. Slightly raising her medium length skirt she showed me how, since her accident, she had never been able to place her foot flat on the ground, only the ball of the foot, which meant that when she stood, her heel was raised. She explained that was why she wore very high heeled shoes, because she did not wish people to think she was lame in any way. By bending her knee a little as she stood, she looked normal enough. Whenever she sat down, however, since her foot would not lie flat, she had perforce to put her leg forward, and with the heel resting, the toes pointed upward.

'This morning I decided to go to Matins,' she continued, 'and suddenly, during the reading of the Lesson, there was a loud crack—I'm sure everyone must have heard it—and my foot, which has been hunched up in my shoe these six years, opened out of its own accord.'

I was silent, recalling an iron gate that once opened of its own accord to set the apostle Peter free to witness to Christ for the rest of his life.

Hannah said, 'You evidently haven't seen me going up and downstairs while I've been here.' This was true, but I hadn't realised it. 'Well,' she grinned, 'for years I have been like a crab, doing it sideways, putting the good foot on a step or stair first, then bringing the other one into position beside it, so to avoid accidents. Fancy, all these years going up and down sideways!'

'And now?' I asked.

'I'll show you,' she said laughingly, and ran in a normal way like any youngster up and down seven or eight steps that led from the house to the garden. Moreover, during her stay she ate the same meals as the rest of us, and that without any pain in her chest or sour taste in her mouth. There was no need for any operation, for her ulcer had been attended to by the Divine Physician.

It was about a week after the initial laying on of hands when once more Hannah called at our home. She looked a trifle embarrassed, but not for long. She opened the conversation by saying, 'I don't know what you'll think of me, but I've come to tell you about my back.'

'Oh, so you did have something wrong with your back after all?' I queried.

'Well, yes, but I'd forgotten all about it,' she said, 'it happened so long ago. I only ever had one child, and he was born thirty-five years ago, but the bottom two vertebrae of my spine were broken when he was born. For a year or so I had a lot of pain, then it went. Could that account for the pain on Sunday?'

'I wouldn't know,' I answered; 'I am more inclined to believe that when you fell down the steps on to the beach you probably did some damage to your back; but who is to know? Only the Holy Spirit whose task it is to manifest Jesus "the same yesterday, today, and for ever".'

Hannah was a joy to be with during those weeks. Her testimony proved a blessing to many. After all, we are not healed to enjoy selfish living, but to witness to the Healing Christ, and so to serve others.

On the last evening of her stay she came to us for one more chat, one more cup of tea. The end of the evening was unexpected. Suddenly she said, 'Will you pray for me just once more?'

'What for?' I asked.

'For the Baptism in the Holy Spirit,' she replied.

No one had ever asked such a thing of me, and I was still needing teaching myself about it. I looked at my wife with an unspoken question.

Lucy said: 'I don't see why not; after all, it is for all those who are afar off, as Simon Peter said at Pentecost.'

So my wife and I laid hands on our friend for the last time, asking Jesus to bestow the free gift of His Spirit, that Hannah might be a better witness for Him. In a few minutes she began to laugh, then cried a little, and laughed again. We took her back to her room under the African star-studded sky, one of us holding a torch to lead the way lest we tripped over the great roots of the mango trees, or stepped on frogs. To say the least, our friend needed our steadying hands, and we laughed so much that I said, 'Now I know what they meant in Jerusalem long ago when at Pentecost mockers said the disciples were filled with new wine.'

She left by train early next day.

A few weeks later we had a letter telling us of her experience. As she sat alone in her compartment en route for Durban, thinking of all the Lord had done for her, she was filled with joy and thanksgiving. Then, suddenly and unexpectedly, from her own lips came in no uncertain manner the sounds of an unknown tongue.

'I don't know what it was,' she wrote, 'but it sounded to me like some African dialect. I knew it was all praises to God, like a lot of Hallelujahs and Hosannas. It went on and on and I felt I couldn't stop it, but as the train drew into the station the tongue ceased as if someone had turned it off like a tap.' She also told us that she had since stood before a meeting of women from her own denomination and given her testimony; and, not least, that having done so, she was able to pray fearlessly before them all in an extemporary way. So the Lord answered fully that short and simple prayer made over her at her first healing service.

Looking back, the mental picture I shall always carry of Hannah is of the day when she came along the hospital stoep as I sat chatting with some of our patients. She was a radiant figure as she approached us, and throwing her arms wide open she cried, 'Oh, Father, I love everybody!'

We all laughed. 'That's right, Hannah,' I said, 'that's what divine healing is all about.'

## *3* **BETTY**

'The years teach much the hours never knew.' I can still recall a day at college when I was taking a degree in Honours Theology and a student asked a question that raised a momentary flicker of interest. Doubtless we were doing New Testament study, possibly the gospel story of Jesus casting out demons from the man who said his name was Legion, and of the ensuing rush of swine over a precipice only to be choked—some two thousand of them—in the sea. This account has given opportunity to countless scholars to discuss and write about the moral issues involved, but both the learned professor and the students were surprised to hear voiced the question, 'Sir, are there really demons?'

The reply came without hesitation, 'Oh no, of course not.' Maybe the smiles on not a few faces encouraged the young man to further the point. 'But, sir, it says so here.' And I can still remember the gist of the professor's words which were meant to put an end to the matter as far as we were concerned: 'Yes, of course, but you must remember that people knew no better in those days. They knew nothing of psychology and psychiatry, and in our time we know very well there are no such beings as demons.' Once more the young man ventured a challenge: 'But, sir, Jesus must have believed there were, because He gave them leave to enter the swine.'

By this time we students sensed something of battle

in the air, and perhaps for that reason alone I well recall the learned professor's reply: 'Oh, no!' he said. 'Jesus knew what was in man, and although He knew there were no such things as demons He had to pretend to accept what was a commonly held belief in His day. If He had let them think He didn't believe in demons, then they wouldn't have believed anything else He taught them.' And that ended the matter—the success of mind over matter, I suppose!—and for the next thirty years the theologian's opinion was pigeon-holed somewhere in my brain, until I came into the ministry of divine healing.

As far as I remember no one during my time of education and preparation for the ministry ever made special note of the Lord's commission as found in St. Luke's gospel (9 : 1, 2), or if they did, no reference was made to divine healing as being something we should be involved in after ordination. We expected to preach, and to visit and pray for the sick of course, but the actual sickness in body and/or mind was the concern of doctors and/or psychiatrists. In His commission Jesus Himself bestowed both power and authority for the work His disciples would have to do. The power is His Spirit; the authority is His name. The first healing miracle that is recorded after Pentecost clearly reveals this (Acts 3 : 4–10).

The task of those commissioned involves four different ministries, distinct yet making up the whole, and when we practise our ministry there must often be some overlapping. It is interesting to note that Luke, a careful historian, puts the deliverance ministry first; as a medical doctor himself he doubtless found the most difficult patients were those either 'oppressed of the devil', or suffering from neuroses, and those who were out of their minds who as often as not were thought of as 'demon-possessed'. Power over demons is one thing, power to cure disease another, preaching the kingdom of heaven is something more, while healing the sick is a ministry involving the whole personality. Nowadays we

26

speak of integrating personality. The sick are more than diseases, they are people who each have a sense-conscious, a God-conscious, and a self-conscious part; or we can say each has a physical body, a human spirit, and is a living soul, the soul being the psyche . . . which is the will, the intellect, the mind, the emotions, and the seat of our human personality.

Since ordination I had been involved in preaching and praying, teaching and counselling. Only after I went to South Africa did I meet the challenge of healing the sick and using the authority and name of Jesus against demons. For this reason I tell the story of Betty, a little six-year-old girl whom Jesus shepherded to me. He had a loving purpose for her, of course, but also for others whom He was to bring to me in the years ahead. Hers is not an isolated case, and perhaps no two cases are exactly alike, though for me, hers was the first in my own experience of the deliverance ministry. I can only give such facts as the mother herself told me, and my own clear recollection of my personal involvement at the time. When you have read the story of Betty you may be able to form your own opinion as to whether or not a demon, or more than one, controlled her . . . whether from within, or from without.

One winter's afternoon I answered the telephone in our house and heard a voice new to me. It was a young mother who said she needed help desperately for her child, Betty. The family attended a Methodist church some sixty miles away, and the minister had suggested she contact our Healing Home though we had never met. He well knew the need, and no doubt felt their problem too much for him, as indeed it had proved for others. The mother gave a lucid account. Betty at the early age of two years had been warded in a neurological ward of a large hospital; the mother worked there now in a secretarial capacity. An electro-encephalogram had revealed at so early an age that the non-dominant side of the brain was not working properly, and there were signs of disturbance in the brain which betokened epileptic fits yet to come. These attacks did come and varied in degree. She was put on medication and at different times had seven various combinations of drugs. Distressing times for the family were relieved by stretches of a few months during which there were no fits. Several years passed and the child was often very difficult, and when school age was reached the specialist advised a wait for one year as Betty's behaviour was unsatisfactory.

When she did start school she was very troublesome. There were times when she ran out of the classroom and made for home, her teacher in pursuit, thereby leaving her class unattended. I gathered the child had already been turned out of two schools. During these schooling periods school psychiatrists and other workers at a neuro-clinic had tried to help, but the child was very unstable. At one time she was put on three drugs at different times of the day; some were taken thrice, and one once. She lost all her inhibitions, and was put in a neuro-surgical ward of a good hospital, where she was taken off all drugs and put on paraldehyde.

Eventually she came out of hospital and started at a Roman Catholic school. The nuns were very helpful, but the child's behaviour was such that her own teacher was in despair. When the mother had called to collect Betty the afternoon she rang me, the teacher had told her that the Reverend Mother, being Headmistress, would like to talk with her after the weekend. The mother felt sure her child was about to be turned away from yet a third school, and that was why she rang me.

An added reason for approaching me was that the specialist wanted to send Betty to a psychiatric unit for intensive care, for experimental treatment . . . but on condition that the parents would promise not to visit the child at all during the period of anything from six to twelve months.

Now a sick child inevitably brings problems to any home, and the enemy Jesus speaks of is an expert at breaking up the harmony of home, even a marriage, and may often use a child in doing so. I was not surprised to hear that the psychiatrists and medical men who had done their best, seemingly with little success, apportioned much of the blame for the child's condition and behaviour to her parents. Maybe they were right, maybe not. The problem was how to save the child—or that is how I saw it—and the home, possibly, from enemy destruction. The mother desired her child to be educated, for she was intelligent. Furthermore, for the child herself to know she had been turned out of three schools was psychologically bad, and she wasn't seven yet. During the long talk on the telephone I tried to keep my mind open to the Holy Spirit.

I felt He was telling me it was a case of demon possession, but how could I tell the mother so, and apart from her story what else had I to go on? She asked me to minister to the child, but after all the years of expert treatment from those skilled in the sciences, what could I do? Very little in the natural, but my work lay in the supernatural, and with God nothing is impossible.

This was no time for sensitivity, so I asked the mother if I could be frank. She said she would prefer me to be so. I had never before faced the problem of telling a mother that I thought maybe her child was controlled by a demon. However, I did so, and after a moment or two of silence she replied: 'Well, as a matter of fact, I've wondered about it more than once myself.'

It was agreed she would bring the child to me on Sunday morning, and that after a talk at our house she would come with Betty to our healing service for ministry. After greeting them on arrival we sent Betty with an older child to have a look round our beautiful estate while her mother chatted with Lucy and me. When they returned we were sitting on the stoep, and I purposely made little advance to Betty, such children always

29

wanting attention anyway. How to get to the stage of actually rebuking the enemy without letting the child know was my main problem; obviously she must not have the slightest idea of what was in our minds. If indeed there was an evil spirit in her, then it would be aware of our intention.

Hands clasped behind her back, she walked round the stoep, and no one was more surprised than I when she unexpectedly sat herself firmly on my lap, threw her arm round my neck, and, linking her hands, seemed as if she was trying to choke me. I had to use real force to pull her arms away in order to breathe. Her face was very near mine, her eyes noticeably showing much of the whites as is not uncommon in epileptics. Perhaps it was just my introduction to the enemy within, but time would tell.

'Well!' I said. 'Not many young ladies sit on my lap unasked, and throw their arms round my neck like that . . and perhaps it's a good thing too!'

She stared into my eyes, saying nothing, as if trying to size me up. I continued, not unkindly, 'While you've been round the gardens your mother has been telling me what strange things you do, naughty things too sometimes; but then, I sometimes do naughty things also, and so does my wife, and your mother and father . . . in fact I rather think it was only Jesus who was never really naughty. And that reminds me; at this time on Sundays you are usually at children's church, aren't you?'

At this she nodded emphatically, and I felt I was being accepted, which was both encouraging and essential. The thought came to me that maybe I could pray for her now. So I suggested that since she was absent from her own church perhaps I could say a prayer for all of us, especially for her, asking Jesus to help us to be kind and good. This was something new, perhaps, for a man in a clerical collar to pray for you while you sat on his lap; anyway, she sat still.

'Now,' I said, 'let's all close our eyes and be quiet for a few moments and I'll put my hand gently on your head while we all sit very still, and after I've talked to Jesus we'll have some tea and cake.' I put my hand on her head and closed my eyes, and in the ensuing moments of silence I rebuked the enemy in the name of Jesus, commanding any demon to leave her, forbidding it to go to anyone else. Opening my eyes I found everyone had theirs closed, except Betty, so I closed mine again, said a simple prayer aloud, and felt I had at least made a start. Never having been taught what to do, one could only do what seemed right.

She was no real trouble in our company, and after refreshment we walked up to our chapel to the normal healing service, where there was a good congregation. During the service she sat quietly enough, but at one point she took my wife's hand in hers and after examining it said in a whisper, 'I could pull hairs out of your hand . . . and it would hurt.' Lucy answered quietly, 'I hope you won't!'; and a little later, holding Lucy's thumb she whispered, 'I could bend your thumb right back, and I could break it!', to which Lucy again replied, in a whisper, 'I hope you won't!' and was thankful she did not attempt it. It was some weeks later that a friend on our staff who at the time had no idea why the child was with us at the service, told me she had been fascinated by the little girl. She said it was her hands that drew her attention, for never once during the service did her hands remain still . . . they were always moving . . . until after she received the laying on of my hands in prayer at the end of the service, and from that moment they were stilled. Actually, it was at that moment I exorcised any spirit for the third time! But I go before my story.

During the early part of the service my mind was occupied with Betty, and I felt none too sure that any spirit that may have been in the child would have left after a silent command from me. Did one have to shout at a demon or didn't one? We are not told explicitly that

Jesus shouted, but then we are not told He ever spoke an exorcism in silence. What did He do regarding the Syrophenician woman's daughter who was delivered from a distance? Such thoughts kept coming, and then I felt I had a brainwave. Of course, it may have been the direction of the Holy Spirit.

At an appropriate moment before the sermon I told everyone to stand: staff, patients and visitors. Then I told them I felt led to exorcise any work of Satan in or around us, and to cast out any evil spirits from our midst. The astonished looks on the faces of some of my co-workers led me to think such a thing had never been done before in quite this way at a public service. Lifting my hands, in loud, strong terms I then bound every evil spirit in our midst and cast them out in Jesus' name. The reaction of the staff I never knew, but I did feel quite a thrill to think I'd done it in a way which the child, presumably, would in no way connect with herself . . . even if she understood a little.

When, however, at the end of the service I found her kneeling with others in front of me at the sanctuary rail I was quite taken aback. Of course the mother didn't know I had exorcised the child twice . . . so what? As I prayed for someone next to Betty I suddenly remembered Jesus asked Peter three times: 'Lovest thou Me?'; and then gave him a command three times. I thought if the Lord could do that to Peter, then I could again command a demon and any of its ilk to clear out 'in the name of Jesus'. So now, a third time, laying my hands on the child, I exorcised, but this time did so in theological terms. She couldn't understand, but since demons have some intelligence or at least more knowledge than perhaps most of us imagine, it/they would hear and understand. No one was more aware than I of the fact that only God's power could heal this child and deliver her from the powers of darkness.

After the congregation had departed I spoke with the parents. Betty explored the chapel meantime. I told them

I felt I had done all I could at this stage, but pointed out that they could bring her for further ministry if they thought it was needed. I said frankly that it had been in the nature of an experiment for me, as I was entirely new to this ministry. On the other hand, whereas others in the medical and allied professions had blamed them largely for the child's behaviour, I had turned the picture upside down or back to front. I said, 'I think she had or has a demon in her, and if so you may well find her behaviour even worse for a day or two than ever before. But, please don't smack her or lose your tempers because if I am right she is not to blame for the extraordinary things she does to upset everyone. She doesn't control this spirit, it controls her, and uses her not least to break up your marriage and home. This is ever the enemy's work. I could be wrong, but time will tell.' I also added that a demon might not necessarily come out immediately, hence I guessed there might well be a battle between the Holy Spirit and the enemy . . . but Jesus has 'all power' so the enemy would have to go.

At this point Betty's patience was presumably exhausted for she forcefully kicked a chair a few yards across the nave. So we moved from the chapel to their car, and though the others were soon seated Betty did not want to go. I think she took a fancy to Lucy and me. She sat rebelliously on the stone step of the general office, elbows on knees, chin cupped in her hands, scowling so heavily that I recalled fairy tales where eyebrows are said to meet the chin. Impervious to persuasion, rebuke or command, her mother had to get out of the car and literally heave her on to the back seat; as they drove away we saw one unhappy little girl glaring at us through the back window. We did not tell the staff what we had been about.

We heard nothing more of the child for two weeks, and then her mother rang me. As soon as I spoke her strong voice boomed in my ear: 'Praise the Lord!' She proceeded to enlighten me as to Betty, but first reminded me how I had warned them she might be difficult that Sunday. Indeed, the rest of that day had been the worst time they had ever known with her; but the tide is often most turbulent before the turn. They were thankful to put her to bed early, and she slept well. Monday morning her husband dressed, left the bedroom but soon returned to say Betty's eyes were noticeably normal. It was too early to tell if she was healed. 'Remember,' her mother said to me, 'I had to meet the Headmistress at the Convent School, and I dreaded it. But Betty was quite good on the way to school, for a change, and as we waited for her teacher—I've always had to take Betty to school and collect her in the afternoon because of the behaviour problem—another nun came along and we exchanged a "Good morning". She was going to pass, but glancing at Betty she stopped in her tracks then said, "Why, whatever's happened to Betty?" "What do you mean?" I asked. She said, "Well, she's different. What have you done to her over the weekend?" This surprising statement recalled the improvement in Betty's eyes, and I blurted out that I'd taken her to you and you had exorcised her. The nun looked somewhat impressed, put her arm round Betty's shoulder and said, "Well, don't you stay, I'm sure she's going to be all right." So I left, not even going to the Reverend Mother.'

Then she went on to say she had not rung before because it had seemed almost too good to be true. As day followed day without any unpleasant outburst to spoil the home, she had delayed until now; and then she said : 'Betty really has been good, but even more than that— sometimes she has been so sweet my husband and I could scarcely believe she was our own little girl.'

There was a silence between us on the phone. I don't think I had ever heard any parent make such a confession. I know tears welled into my eyes, and I thought, 'the Devil *is* a devil to attack even little children'.

She continued by saying this was the happiest day of her life, even including her wedding day, and that was why she had at last rung me. Behind her were years of heartache and unhappiness, not least stormy interviews with teachers, a mother battling for her child under most trying circumstances. 'Today,' she said, 'I took Betty to school as usual and her teacher, who had almost despaired of her, said, "Why do you bring her to school?" and I told her I had always had to because she was so badly behaved en route. Her teacher said, "But she is no trouble now, she's completely changed; in fact, I've put her among the naughty children in the class to discipline them! You don't need to bring her or collect her from school any more." ' And then Betty's mother said, 'I never thought to hear any schoolteacher say such a thing of my child. It is a miracle. Thank God.'

Later on I was to receive Betty's school report signed by her own teacher, and at the bottom of it beside the word CONDUCT were two sweet words, VERY GOOD. Unwittingly, perhaps, the nun had set her seal to His work of grace.

Time passed and we heard no more until one day mother and child arrived to pay us a short visit. One thing stands out in my mind from that visit. We had at the time a kindly man whose life had been ruined by the enemy. He was an able man and had been a bookkeeper in earlier days; now he was an alcoholic. Loved by his family, and he loved them too, his presence could finally no longer be tolerated, and so he was in a real sense 'outcast'.

After Betty had left he told me how she had wandered into the office where he was busy at the books, though his mind was almost continually on his wife and family many hundreds of miles away. He talked with her and maybe she sensed his need, for children often do. It was hot, and he had no jacket on, and she suddenly put her hand out and began to stroke his arm gently, as if in sympathy. It was a long time since anyone had caressed him, and it moved him greatly. When he told me about it, not knowing Betty's story at all, he said,

35

'What a sweet little girl, and she seemed to know I had a basinful of trouble. She is like an angel.'

It so happened that a new manager had come to our Healing Home. He was not convinced that supernatural healings took place; so I suggested Lucy should ask for a few written accounts of healing that had taken place since we had worked at the Home. One of the people she wrote to was Betty's mother. I was rather surprised when we had no answer for several weeks, feeling that if Betty was troublesome again her mother would have brought her to me.

Then, once more a phone call, which serves to make a fitting climax to this story. Her mother apologised for not answering Lucy's request but said she had been wondering about Betty's brain, which had revealed disturbances long ago. There was no doubt about the change in Betty, though like any other child she could at times be naughty, but not as in the past of course. Talking it over with a friend who was a headmaster of a school, he said, 'Why don't you ask the surgeon to see Betty once more and to take all the tests again, and then you'll know the answer to your question.' Strangely enough, the idea hadn't entered her head, but she mentioned it to the surgeon and he agreed. Betty was put through the various up-to-date tests and a day or two later her mother stood before the doctor in anticipation.

He had before him all the evidence. His words to her were: 'I have all the results here . . . and I have to tell you that the non-dominant side of the brain is working quite normally. There are no other signs of disturbance in the brain, and I see no reason why we should expect any more epilepsy.' Then he concluded, 'In fact, woman, it's quite unbelievable!'

Some months later, just before we returned to work in England, I had just ended an eight-day mission in a city church. Standing at the west door the congregation filed past, many of them stopping for a moment of farewell. Some had become our very good friends, and we shall never forget their hospitality and prayerful backing.

Suddenly I was surprised to find two smiling faces before me. I had not been aware of Betty and her mother among the large congregation. They had come to wish Lucy and me 'Bon Voyage'. It was good to see them. As her mother and I were talking I suddenly became aware of a tugging at my surplice sleeve. Looking down I had quite a shock for a second; Betty, demanding my attention once more, looked astonishingly different. In a moment or two she had popped some ugly celluloid teeth into her mouth, and two bulging celluloid eyes stood out like marbles over her own—she gave me quite a fright!

'Betty!' her mother cried in shocked tone. 'Take those out at once; don't you know you're in God's House?' Betty quickly removed them; she and I exchanged a grin of understanding. To her mother I said, 'Don't worry, she's all right, bless her. And remember, high spirits are never evil spirits, thank God!'

# 4 DOUGLAS

It was after eight o'clock and Sister had given the night nurses their instructions at our European hospital. Now she was going off duty. Looking at her as we chatted for a few minutes I noticed how tired she was, for her work was exacting. I told her of a letter I had received that morning from another sister, at present in England, who might possibly decide to come and join her; we were under-staffed. It was a ray of hope in a somewhat dark picture, for there was a dearth of qualified nursing sisters in the province. Our problem was not only to maintain the work on hand, but also to satisfy the vigilant Health Authorities as to staffing requirements. True, shortage of trained staff was a problem most hospitals faced, but we could not hold out the tempting salaries offered by provincial hospitals. We had comparatively little help from the State or the Church, for our work among Europeans was mainly of a charitable nature, neither state nor diocesan. (The Province met the cost of our work among Zulu children.) Thus we had to rely on those many intercessors who wished to further the work of divine healing; their monetary gifts as well as their constant prayers were essential to our work. Even so, our staff was comprised of Christians who were called of God to this work, and so were willing to come, often from lands many thousands of miles away, for a very small salary. Furthermore, some of our African

38

staff were fine and capable workers, without whom we could not have continued to provide so much for needy people; all in all, I marvelled at times how the Lord kept the work going so well.

More than once we thought we had found another sister, but for one or another reason she never came. Now, with a possible recruit in mind, I suddenly decided to go to Durban the next day as the Chairman of our Board must be consulted. Then and there I picked up the phone, and we agreed to meet at nine o'clock next morning. It was at that point that God began to work a miracle, though as I put the receiver down I was quite unaware of it.

One of the snags about community life is that we can be too near each other for too long—our faults are writ large for others to see—and the enemy is ever active to use our weaknesses to create disharmony and so to spoil every work that would and should give glory to Jesus. Moreover, living as we had to in close proximity with sick and burdened people, some of whom were very difficult because they were emotionally or mentally unbalanced, there were times when we longed to get away if only for a short break; this was not always possible, but the need was felt.

On this occasion I could combine my brief visit to the Board Chairman with an afternoon visit to a general hospital, at which I was a frequent visitor to such patients as would ask me to minister to them prayerfully. One of our own patients, a man whom we had recently taken to this hospital for major surgery, would doubtless be pleased to see me; his family never visited him.

Thus it was that next morning I dressed at five-thirty with a sense of elation; ever since I had been in Natal I had promised myself a day on the beautiful beach at Durban, a real day of relaxation, and I optimistically put on flannels and a sports shirt, even taking a towel and bathing trunks for a swim. No need to wear a clerical collar, I told myself, for I would visit my patient during afternoon visiting hours. It so happened the hospital overlooked the beach. Several of our patients also came for a day's shopping, and a nurse to care for one of them, and as we drove through the main gates I think we all felt a sense of freedom. The sunshine added to the beauty of the north coast scenery, and when at last the view opened out to the blue of the Indian Ocean we really felt we were in a new world. Living amid sugar-country, though only fifty miles from a fine city, we sometimes felt it might have been five hundred; and though I love the country, as well as the seaside, I am really a town dweller.

Arriving at an hour when most people would be having their breakfast, we each went our own way, and soon I was seated in a restaurant with a table to myself; around me Indian waiters were busy at their task. Scanning the menu was encouraging, for in South Africa one could get so much more for one's money: always a consideration when having to budget carefully. Before I had finished my meal, the most English-like city in the country began to pulsate, the throb of the traffic was more noticeable; Durban was shaking off the slumbers of the night.

The pre-arranged meeting with the Chairman was held and we parted, but no sooner had he disappeared from sight than I thought something I had said might be mis-construed, so I felt I'd better put him in the clear at once. I knew he worked in an office nearby, but not exactly where. Entering a kiosk outside the G.P.O. I rang his wife who gave me his office telephone number; as we chatted I heard the high-pitched tones of an Indian lady in the next booth, and on the other side a woman had two calls: the kiosks not being completely enclosed as in England. Then I rang my Chairman friend who had just arrived in his office.

Turning to come out and make my way to the beach, I found my way barred by a European woman from the next kiosk. Holding up a scrap of paper on which a

40

telephone number was written, she asked if I would get through for her as her machine did not seem to be working. I assured her someone had just made two calls there, so perhaps the line was only engaged. She said it was not so, for the line was dead.

I hadn't the necessary *tikki*, so asked if she had one, and she opened her handbag to find one. As she looked down, a sudden flash of recognition came to mind; I had surely seen her before but couldn't think who she was. She handed me the *tikki*, and I asked, 'Haven't we met before somewhere?' She scrutinised my face for a moment or two then said, 'I don't think so.' I groped in my mind, which has never been good at remembering names though more successfully faces. I guessed her age to be a little less than my own, noting that she had a pleasant appearance altogether, while at the same time trying to catch an elusive memory. It would be awful, I thought, if I had made a mistake. I tried another tack. 'Would you know me if I had a collar on back to front?' I asked, and with a smile drew an imaginary one round my neck.

She echoed : 'Collar back to front . . . ?' A momentary smile flitted across her face which she quickly checked as she took on a sterner look. 'No, I don't know you,' she said brusquely, 'and I've never seen you before.' She evidently felt I was being somewhat familiar, to say the least. But happily for me, at that moment I felt sure I knew where we had met; only once, and then quite briefly for twenty minutes or so, and that almost two years ago; I could, of course, still be wrong.

'It's a long time ago,' I told her, 'but it's all coming back to mind. I met you on the top floor of the Head Office of the Mission to Lepers, Bloomsbury Square, London : some six thousand miles away. I recall the things you said at the time, and a particular story you told me about your missionary deputation work. You were so tired after a 200-mile train journey and had to speak on arrival at a south coast resort. You said you felt like a wet sack—I'd never heard that expression before. As you addressed the meeting the Holy Spirit took over and your listeners both laughed and wept. At the end of the week's work, an old lady put a brown paper parcel in your hands at the station saying its contents were for the work you represented—and how much your first talk had moved her. You later counted two hundred and five one-pound notes inside the parcel.'

Her face lit up with pleasure when I finished speaking: 'What a memory!' she cried, 'and I do recall now that you came into the room at the end of an afternoon at the Mission. I should never have known you. What are you doing in Durban?' I told her in a few words, and she quickly told me she was staying at the Worldwide Evangelization Crusade House a couple of miles away. I had not known there was such a centre in Durban. She and her husband were moving on to Australia and Tasmania as his task was to place missionaries in various parts. She had come to a shipping office to book their passage, but needed more information, so had to contact her husband or go all the way back home for the particulars.

Then I inserted the coin and dialled the number, but there was no sound. I tried a second time, but the line was indeed dead. 'Never mind,' she said. 'If you can spare the time you must come in the bus with me to W.E.C. House and then you can meet my husband too.' We were so elated at meeting each other in this way; home, after all, was six thousand miles distant, and in each other we felt a touch of home. We talked so excitedly in the bus that everyone seemed intensely interested in us. We were going further from the beach, but that didn't matter now.

When we arrived, I had a warm welcome and accepted an invitation to lunch, and met her husband and the staff. They were quite convinced that there had been nothing wrong with the phone for they had used it often for outgoing and incoming calls. Looking back, I believe the Lord silenced that line for His own purposes. Because of this, I never had my day on the beach: 'Man proposes, God disposes.'

Over lunch I answered their questions about my own work in the Healing Home, and since they too loved the Lord they rejoiced to hear some of His mighty works. We lingered at the table after lunch was over. One young man, Terence, suddenly asked me if I had read in the evening paper a few days before of a sixteen-year-old schoolboy named Douglas who, according to report, had tried to take his life by taking a massive dose of tablets. He had been epileptic from childhood, and had asked God to heal him in vain, so had attempted to end it all. I said we never saw an evening paper as we lived far from any shops, so had not heard this sad account. Terence said: 'I'd never heard of the boy before, but as soon as I read the account, the Lord put a burden of prayer on my heart for him.' In fact, Terence said he had been so burdened that after praying for two days and nights he was moved to go to the hospital, thinking he might pray for the boy there. The W.E.C. both believes in and practises the scriptural injunction to heal the sick; Terence was a W.E.C. worker. Even so, I marvelled that such a young man could pray so earnestly for a lad he had never even met.

He continued: 'When I arrived, he was still alive but unconscious. His mother was there and I explained why I had come, and asked if I might pray for him; but she refused.'

'Refused,' I echoed. 'But why?'

'Well, apparently because they are Anglican and I am not,' he answered.

I had never heard of such a thing and said so. Terence paused, then added: 'It seems they have many Anglican friends praying for him and the Bishop of Zululand has flown all the way to Durban to pray at the bedside, so his mother said, as Douglas comes from Zululand. I guess she thought my prayers wouldn't come anywhere near his.'

It seemed incredible to me, and in a brief silence I tried to understand the mother's attitude. Terence continued: 'I haven't stopped praying, of course, but the boy has now been unconscious for three days and nights. Are you staying in Durban a few days?'

'No, only a few hours,' I answered, but reading his mind I asked, 'Why?'

'Well,' he said, with some eagerness, 'since the Lord uses you in this work of healing, I wonder if you would go and pray for Douglas. You're Anglican too.'

'Of course,' I said with a smile, 'and if his mother is there then I'll have to tell her I'm a priest: it might help. Apart from my visit to the beach I intended going to that hospital anyway, for Douglas is where one of our patients is awaiting a possible operation. When I think of how I came to be here I'm sure the Lord has arranged it, and I believe He means me to be a link in a chain; remember, I am not a healer, but He is.'

Terence was joyful: 'That's fine,' he said, 'and while you are there I'll be on my knees here backing you up.'

A few minutes later a lady missionary at our table led me to her car and drove to the hospital, passing the lovely beach where so many were enjoying themselves, though I had no regrets at not being among them. First I went to our own patient and was able to minister to him. Then I made my way upstairs to another ward, a nurse directing me to the farthest corner from the door. I could see the prone figure of Douglas who was still unconscious, the drip feed doing its work, while beside him sat two women. One was small, dark, pale and dressed entirely in black. I was to learn she was his mother, a widow, and Douglas her only son; the other, blonde and silent, sat on a small bench provided for visitors. There were visitors talking round other beds, but here there was the drama of silent waiting. Already uncon-

44

scious three days and nights, no one could tell whether he would survive, for the longer one is unconscious after such an overdose of drugs the less likely is it that one will recover.

I had never before faced quite such a situation, and knew it might prove difficult. However, knowing that attack is the best form of defence, I rather breezed into their company and sat down beside the lady on the bench. 'Well, well, so this is Douglas!' I said brightly, as each looked at me in astonishment. I then explained how I had been to the G.P.O. and had met a friend from England, and how later I had heard about Douglas. I told of Terence too, and frankly told the mother I felt she had treated him somewhat ungraciously in refusing to let him pray.

They listened in silence, until I ended by saying, 'That's why I am here. Terence is still praying for your son, and I am hoping you will let me pray now that I'm here.'

His mother, the little lady in black, said 'No, thank you; you see, we are Anglicans.'

'I understand that,' I said, 'and I'm an Anglican too; in fact, I'm an Anglican priest.'

'A priest?' she echoed in surprise. She looked me up and down, doubtless coming to her own conclusion regarding my green flannels and sports shirt; I hardly looked a cleric.

'Oh, indeed,' I said cheerfully, and for the second time that day drew an imaginary collar round my neck. 'We don't always wear it, you know . . . and I never do when I go on a beach to laze in the sun.'

I explained who I was, where I worked in the healing ministry, and something of the way Jesus heals today. After we had talked awhile I was struck by their negative attitude and hopeless outlook, revealed both in their faces and speech. I said they could be more of a hindrance to Douglas than a help. Furthermore, in their present state of unbelief they might even prevent the boy's recovery. As a parish priest, I told them, I had discovered that it is possible for an unconscious person to be adversely affected by our negative statements.

In answer to my second request to pray, assuring them I should not be either long or loud, his mother said, 'No, thank you. You see we have many Anglican friends already praying for my son.'

I was already aware of the fact, though she didn't know it. I countered: 'I'm pleased to hear it; the more prayer the better, but you don't seem to have any expectant faith, and without it you can't help him. If you only have a crumb of faith you must offer it up to Jesus to add to His own, and then He will use His and yours to restore Douglas.'

There was stalemate. I turned the conversation to other things for a time, but eventually asked for the third time if I could pray for Douglas. Her refusal was polite but firm; it also carried an air of triumph, as one might lay down the ace of trumps to finalise victory: 'No. There is no need for you to pray for my son, for the Bishop of Zululand has kindly flown all the way to Durban for the purpose of praying for him.'

Aware that the sands were running out, I said spiritedly, 'Fine. I'm quite sure the Bishop is a far better man than I am, or he wouldn't be a bishop; moreover, his praying is probably much better than mine. But the next time you meet him I want you to look him straight in the eye and say, "My Lord, did you ever have a specific call to the ministry of divine healing?" And because he's an honest man he will say, "No, I didn't." Well, I did! God called me into this work and brought me all the way from London to Durban, and how do you know He didn't do it for the express purpose of raising up your son? You don't know! And how do you know it was not the power of the Bishop's prayer and the prayers of your other Anglican friends which opened the way for me to come to your son's bedside today?

46

You don't know. Now, are you, or are you NOT, going to let me pray for your son?'

Looking her straight in the eye I waited . . . make no mistake, this was a battle with the enemy even if we weren't conscious of it . . . and then she looked across to her friend and raised her eyebrows with the unspoken question. Her friend, silently, nodded her head. 'Very well, you may,' said his mother.

This was His victory. I asked her to move a little to enable me to lay one hand on the boy's head, and I took his wrist with the other and uttered a short prayer only loud enough for them to hear. I felt some elation at the victory, but even as I prayed with half my mind, as it were, so the other half was speaking to me: 'This is a rotten prayer after all that battle!'—or, maybe, it was the enemy.

Douglas remained unconscious. I turned and looked at his mother, and a strange thing happened. In a flash I thought of the widow of Nain, and she the widowed mother of an only son. As a young man, this miracle had always moved me most. Quick as thought there came a new experience. I heard a short rush as of wind over my head, which passed through me from head to foot. In a moment I was filled with compassion, not for the boy, whom I didn't know, who didn't even want to live, but for his mother. How harsh I must have seemed to her, but what else could I have done? I now spoke, and in speaking heard the change of tone myself: 'Thank you for letting me pray for your son.' I hesitated a moment, then heard myself add: 'And now I will tell you something: your son will be healed.' Without a moment's hesitation I turned and asked her friend, 'What day is it?' I had no idea as to why I should ask it. 'It's Friday,' came the reply. 'Of course, thank you,' I said. 'Silly of me to forget.' Turning to the mother there came a moment of revelation: 'Friday—Sunday; Good Friday—Easter; death—life.' With not the slightest hesitation I said, 'Your son will be healed. Douglas will wake

47

up three days from now, on Sunday.' I could scarcely believe my own ears.

'Thank you!' she replied, and to my 'Good afternoon' she said, 'Goodbye', but I was already on my way out.

It was brilliant sunshine outside, but even before I left the hospital grounds my mind was full of thoughts tumbling one over another. Someone was saying, 'How dare you say such a thing to her? Don't you remember that little brown booklet you read immediately after you were called to this work, and how you were told *never* to tell anyone whether a patient would live or die—that's only God's prerogative!' Indeed, I had forgotten all about that little book until now, but it was true. I had said things that were only His prerogative to say . . . how awful! And supposing Douglas died today, or tomorrow . . . how harsh a thing to have said to a tragic mother.

Suddenly I stopped in the grounds, and looking up spoke aloud and in no uncertain manner: 'God . . . You brought me here! . . . You put those words on my lips! I would never have said such a thing in all my life. You made me meet Terence. You brought me to Douglas. I'm not going to listen to all this talk. In your Word you say you will honour them that honour you. So be it. I'm putting Douglas in your hands right now, and I'm not taking any more responsibility for him. He's in your hands, not mine.'

And so to rejoin my friends from the Healing Home, and as we sped homeward I knew there was one lad lying unconscious in his hospital bed, while a few miles away another was still on his knees in prayer.

On Sunday morning I told of Friday's strange events. No one fidgeted during that address. Immediately after service one of our elderly patients came to tell me she knew Douglas and his mother well; indeed, his mother was an old friend. She said she would be sure to get a letter from another lady, a mutual friend in Zululand, who would tell her all about him. The next morning the letter came, and told us much. So God graciously filled in the gaps.

When found unconscious in a dying condition, the boy was rushed to hospital in Zululand, where they used a stomach pump and did all they could to save his life. Then they contacted a sugar farmer who gladly allowed the use of his private plane for them to take the boy to Durban to a more modern hospital in an endeavour to restore him. His condition was critical. In the plane, apart from the pilot, there were only the boy, the doctor and a nurse. It was as the plane flew over Zululand that Douglas died. Watching every breath his patient drew, the doctor could hardly be mistaken. To the nurse he said: 'We're too late. We've lost him . . . he's gone! Tell the pilot to bring the plane down.' To say the least, it was terribly disappointing after their efforts to save him. The nurse looked at the lad . . . and suddenly bent down and took up a syringe and quickly prepared an injection and gave it. They watched . . . and shortly, the pulse began to beat faintly once more: thus Douglas had arrived in Durban.

In our chapel on Sunday morning I had asked for prayer for Douglas . . . not that I should be proved right . . . but that God's will for him should be fulfilled. It is not His will that we take life, be it our own or another's. As to an attempted suicide by a boy because his own prayer to God for healing had seemingly never been answered, this could not be God's will either.

The day following the receipt of the letter from Zululand I went to Durban, this time to conduct a healing service in the afternoon. Wondering about Douglas, I decided to go to the hospital at a quiet time when the doctors would have finished their morning rounds, yet before lunch was served. Climbing the flight of stairs once more, I found the glass ward doors open for air to circulate; it was a very hot day. Looking down the long ward I saw Douglas, not lying under the drip feed this time, but sitting up having a haircut from an Indian barber! I breathed a silent 'Thank you, Father.'

The barber began packing his things, and moved to another patient. I shook hands with Douglas and told him I had been to visit him on Friday. He thanked me, adding that he didn't know me. So I told him who I was, and how I had spoken with his mother and her friend. I said, 'Douglas, I told your mother you would wake up on Sunday . . . when did you wake?' He said, 'I don't really know, but they're very kind to me here.'

I beckoned to a nurse and told her I had prayed for Douglas on Friday, and that I had told his mother he would be healed and would wake up on Sunday. Her eyes widened. I asked her, 'When did he wake up?' and then she unwittingly asked exactly the same question I had asked on Friday, 'What day is it?' 'It's Tuesday,' I said. 'Of course,' she acquiesced, 'how silly of me.' Then, concentrating a moment or two she said in an awed voice, 'Yes! . . . it *was* Sunday when he woke.'

Before leaving, I was able to have a word—and give a testimony—to his doctor; then I prayed once more for the boy, and after three days he returned to school. I heard later that he had an epileptic fit immediately he crossed the threshold of the school hostel.

Visiting his school later, I was able to tell his head-master the experiences I had had concerning Douglas.

Several months passed, and one morning my scripture reading was the story of the healing of the lad who had been epileptic since childhood; Jesus cast out a spirit in answer to the father's prayer . . . 'Lord, I believe, help thou my unbelief.' Believing the Lord was guiding me, I rang the headmaster and asked if I might come and minister to Douglas once more, this time to exorcise a demon of epilepsy, and anoint him with oil according to the scripture in James 5. He acquiesced.

A week later I met Douglas for the last time, and ministered to him in private. Chatting with the Head afterwards he said: 'I don't think you knew how ill

Douglas was when you first met him.'

'Well, I know he had been unconscious three days.'

'No! I didn't mean that. I meant his epilepsy.'

'I had only heard he had been epileptic since child-hood.'

'Yes, he had been ill for years. But at the time you met him, at that phase in his life, Douglas was having ten to fifteen fits and turns every day of his life.'

I was appalled: small wonder he had tried to end it.

From the day of his anointing, he began to improve in his school work. Each year, his mother's friend at the Healing Home sends us a greeting at Christmas, as we left for England six months after I first saw the boy, and she always writes, 'Douglas is doing fine'. As for the epilepsy he never had another fit from the day of his exorcism and anointing. To God be all the glory.

# 5  PHILIP

It was Saturday night. The spacious lounge was filled
with patients and visitors, mostly chatting to each other
against a background of music coming from a record
player of dubious age. Several members of staff were
also relaxing in the social atmosphere as a relief to the
normal busy routine of their working week. Some of the
older folk who were spending the rest of their days in
the Home had already occupied their favourite arm-
chairs, while the younger ones were playing innocent
games at tables in a far corner.

Coming into the room, I was surprised to find the
Home Manager with a small group of newcomers who
had arrived that evening; surprised because, in my two-
year period of office, the managers usually avoided the
Saturday night lounge gatherings, doubtless regarding
that side of the work as the responsibility of the Warden.
I was introduced to a man of middle age, Philip, who
said he had come to spend the last week of his holidays
with us. He proved to be a pleasant, rather quiet family
man, and we became friends. I knew nothing of him and
learnt later he had rung up just in time for the manager
to bring him from the city when he went to collect the
others by car. Two things gave me the clue as to why he
had come to our Healing Home when most men would
have gone to some hotel, especially as he had only one
week left of his summer holiday. The first was the strong

smell of brandy that greeted me as I greeted him. Because we sometimes had patients who were alcoholics, no liquor was allowed on the premises, and our African staff were strictly enjoined not to bring alcohol to any patient, no matter what the bribe, on pain of dismissal. The second thing was that while I was speaking to the newcomer the manager, standing behind him, raised his hand to his mouth as if tossing down a drink. Philip's problem was in fact just that.

The next morning he came to the early Communion service for he was a member of the Church of the Province. I had no conversation with him that Sunday as far as I recall, but he attended the later healing service and came forward for the laying on of hands with prayer. I selected my words carefully, not wishing to embarrass him, for his problem was a personal matter and not one to be divulged to others except he chose to do it himself. Yet how often in the healing ministry one realises it is not so much what we say, as what the Holy Spirit does, that matters.

On Monday morning we came out of the dining room together and I invited him to come to my study for a chat at ten o'clock, for he obviously needed counselling. He gladly accepted and told me briefly his story.

His life had been content enough until several years ago. He had a steady but rather poorly paid job, a good wife, and two children, at that time in their teens. As a family it had always been their practice to worship regularly at the parish church; theirs was a happy home. Then, possibly because the cost of living was rising and he was refused any increase in salary, he became troubled at his inability to provide luxuries that his youngsters wanted.

He had been accustomed to meet his men friends for a drink of an evening on his way home from work. They were a small set of cronies who usually met at the same time each day in the same public house, and after a drink or two went home to their evening meal. It could be said that this was social drinking; also, the humid heat made men thirsty.

Philip loved his wife and youngsters; he had been a good husband and father. Now, he began to change. He drank more to bolster himself up. At church they had agreed to pay so much per annum under the stewardship scheme, but soon he fell short of this promise; it added to his burden of conscience, and their regular church attendance began to wane. His quiet reserve may have been maintained outwardly, but a sense of failure made him irritable, and he began to drink spirits instead of beer. To his family he became quite a different person, and the growing youngsters couldn't understand what had happened to their father whom they had always loved. Their mother began to find empty brandy bottles hidden in the most silly places, even under cushions. The enemy who comes to steal and destroy (John 10:10) was in; the peace of a happy home was gone. Fortunately, Philip's wife was wise. She was able to talk to him without scolding, trying to understand the reasons for this unexpected change in him, but anxiety tore at her patience, and prayer seemed unavailing.

Knowing of the Healing Home she tried to persuade Philip to go there for help, but ostensibly as a visitor, for part of his holiday; not only had the money for any family holiday gone down his throat, but if he was not soon set free from this bondage to alcohol he might well lose his job. At the Home maybe he would receive a miracle of God's healing grace. Philip agreed. Four weeks slipped by, however, for it was one thing to see the wisdom of it but another to actually go and reveal your need, and your shame, to some unknown parson. It was more than he could face. So the battle waged within him if not around him. Fear paralysed him.

God's timing is perfect. The Saturday evening newspaper comes out on Saturday morning, and on that last but one Saturday of his holiday Philip stayed at home while his wife went shopping. Opening the paper

54

he saw in one column the regular Saturday feature, a sermon: the heading, 'Divine Healing'. It was written by an American priest in a curacy many miles away. Philip read it. When his wife returned he told her he felt God would heal him if he went to the Healing Home. So he rang and asked if there was room for him for one week. The manager picked him up that afternoon.

A churchgoer all his life, no one had ever introduced Philip to the idea of a Quiet Time, when after prayer one could sit and listen to God, writing down one's thoughts just as they came. In counselling I explained the process. He agreed to try it with me. Was it not strange that we both had an idea that had never before entered our heads? He read out his guidance: 'Ask your wife to come and join you here.' I had written the same words. The fact of this elated him, but he said, 'She'll never come!'

'You're wrong,' I said, 'for whatever the difficulties, God will remove them . . . she'll come all right.'

During our time of sharing he then surprised me by telling me that on the previous day, at the Sunday healing service, when I had prayed over him with my hands on his head, his whole body had seemed to be full of electric currents. I had felt nothing. Again, what we may feel is not important, and what matters is what the Holy Spirit does. Even so, I was knowledgeable enough in this work to feel he must surely have received new life in place of the old, a healing perhaps; only time would tell.

The following day Philip had his own Quiet Time and he heard a clear direction as he sat waiting for thoughts to write down on his pad: 'My son, always listen to me. Be not afraid. Mary will come.' How gracious is God when we seek Him and His will. In all Philip's experience he had never known the reality of the presence of God as he did that week. He was positive he was delivered already from his weakness.

Mary, his wife, came. Very troubled at first, she stayed in our own home where we could teach her, too, to listen to God. She couldn't believe Philip was healed, yet could not deny he was seemingly changed in several ways. Strength had replaced weakness, and he was confident. Not least, in a few days he had put on weight which fear and guilt had unnaturally reduced in past months; even his face had filled out.

At prayers on Friday, in the open air before the Zulu nurses at the Children's Hospital, he stood and gave his testimony to the deliverance he had received from Jesus —he felt no desire for alcohol; how we praised God!

The week ended. On Saturday morning Philip and Mary sat with us on our stoep for a time of prayer and praise before they took their leave, but Mary was still uneasy. No wonder! The nightmare of the past few years had been grim for her. She had hoped he might be healed, but her prayers had scarcely been expectant.

Over our last cup of tea after our prayer time had ended, Mary revealed her fears as she said somewhat timidly, 'Now, Philip, when you come home from work next week you must go the long way round.'

'Why is that?' I asked.

'Well,' she replied, 'there are two ways in which he can get home from work. If he takes the longer way he will avoid going to his favourite pub, and then he won't meet his pals and be tempted to drink.'

Philip and I spoke together, much the same words: 'That's not necessary . . . the healing is done, completed!' This, understandably, she could not accept.

Two weeks later we visited the town where they lived and we rang Mary from a friend's home. She was so excited as she told how Philip had gone the usual way home from work, stopping with his friends in his old haunt. To their surprise he told them courageously of his deliverance. He drank orange juice. Nothing smug about him, just grateful to God for being made a new man. Mary said: 'And the wonderful thing is that not one of them scoffed at him. They all accepted what he said, and several of them, seeing the change in him, his courage instead of the old fears, said they wished they had what he had. One or two of them actually congratulated him and shook him by the hand.'

Over the ensuing period of almost two years we met the family often—and several times I had a chat with Philip. On the last occasion, as we walked together in a lovely park, in answer to a gentle question he answered, 'Oh, yes. Things are going well. We go to church regularly. As for the drink . . . well, I don't visit my old haunt much, and if I do, I chat with my friends, even over a glass of beer occasionally, but I never touch spirits, nor do I have any desire to.'

In a few moments, as it were, God had worked the miracle. Self-control and self-respect, conscious and unconscious witness to others of Jesus' delivering power, and renewed health of body, mind and spirit, had all been attended to by supernatural power and grace. 'It is not by any might or force of man, but by MY Spirit, saith the Lord of hosts.'

# 6  CORDELIA

At periodic intervals, all members of the nursing staff at our Zulu Children's Hospital had to undergo medical tests including x-rays, to make sure they themselves were fit to nurse these one-time TB children. There was one such occasion during our stay when a very pleasant young staff nurse named Ada was found to have a patch on her lung which necessitated her going to a city hospital for treatment. We all liked this girl and felt very sorry for her, but were reassured soon afterwards when it was discovered to be no more than an old scar from the disease which she must have had some years ago without knowing it! Ada was well enough in herself, and did not spend more than several months resting and having treatment before she came back to work once more among our Zulu children. Ada had proved herself an excellent staff nurse, and her sense of humour made her generally popular. While with us she had learnt that miracles do take place through the prayer of faith.

When she entered the African hospital for treatment she shared a small private room with an African nursing sister named Cordelia. (For some years Cordelia had worked on the staff there, but was now herself a patient.) This proved a happy arrangement, for both girls were Roman Catholics, and they quickly became friends. Ada was a great comfort and help to Cordelia who had been fighting a losing battle against tuberculosis for some time. The lady doctor responsible for Cordelia was a Scottish Presbyterian; and for the purposes of my story I'll call her Dr Margaret. She had worked untiringly but with little success for improvement in Cordelia's condition. In addition to Cordelia's doctor, whom we did not know at all, there was also another lady doctor who regularly visited our Zulu children in an official capacity, and she had become our friend; she was also based at this city hospital. I shall call her Dr Ray.

Lucy and I were just about to go away for our summer holiday to the south coast of Natal when our American matron asked if we would go and visit Ada and minister to her and her room-mate Cordelia. This was the first time we had heard of Cordelia, but apparently Ada had been talking to her of the healings that had taken place at our own two hospitals, European and African, and had encouraged her to accept ministry from us. By letter, Ada gave us to understand that Cordelia's plight was very serious. Dr Margaret had hoped finally to build up Cordelia's strength sufficiently to enable her to undergo an operation for the removal of one lung, both being affected by the disease. This had proved impossible, however, for though they had tried various treatments this girl in her twenties had grown steadily worse.

Ada, meantime, had been encouraging Cordelia to look to Jesus, the Divine Physician, for a miracle of healing, and this she had summoned her faith to do.

As Lucy and I were due to go away on the Monday and the matter was urgent, Matron drove us to see both girls on the previous Sunday afternoon. On arrival we first saw Ada; she was looking well and was very thrilled to see us. Cordelia, however, had been moved into the next room on her own; her condition was so bad that I don't think they held out any hope of her recovery. But even so, she was getting the best of care and attention, and on her own she could rest more quietly.

After praying for Ada we went with her to see Cordelia for the first time. I shall never forget her appearance. She was propped up against the pillows, and as we entered she gave us a grateful smile, but even to do that caused great beads of perspiration to come on her forehead and face, a face that was no longer brown but rather a greyish colour. I was at once reminded of photographs we had seen of Belsen victims soon after the last war. Cordelia's skin was stretched tightly over the bones of her finely chiselled face, which seemed now to be nothing more than a frame from which stared two great eyes. Even so, I felt that in health she must have been singularly beautiful. Almost the slightest movement or even effort to talk seemed to exhaust her. We did not, therefore, remain long with her, nor was there any need to. We could do very little, we knew that, but with God nothing is impossible.

I explained simply that we would all three of us lay our hands upon her, and prayer to Jesus would be made for her healing. The actual ministry took only a few minutes, and soon afterwards we left: incidentally, Cordelia had prayerfully prepared herself for this ministry. She was very appreciative of our coming and gave us a wonderful smile as we departed. But we were a very serious group when we closed the door behind us. Next day, Lucy and I went on holiday, and from time to time remembered her in prayer and wondered how she was.

We were away a month, and a week or so after our return we suddenly had an urgent S O S message from Cordelia's own Dr Margaret who, we learned later, had been away at the time of our visit so had known nothing of it for a while. Our Matron now informed us that our mutual friend Dr Ray, on a recent visit to our Zulu hospital, had told her what happened at the city hospital only a couple of weeks after our visit. She had been sitting at lunch in the staff room when she became aware that others were talking animatedly about Cordelia. She pricked up her ears, for she knew we three had visited the girl. There was some elation among the staff, for Cordelia had not only improved, but had put on three pounds in weight, and that for the first time for months! This was a miracle. No one could even pretend to have an answer to it. Consequently, our friend Dr Ray found herself in the position of having to say something about us, and divine healing; normally the very idea would have been out of the question. However, she plucked up courage enough to say quietly: 'I think I know why Cordelia has put on weight, and is gaining ground.' Whereupon Dr Margaret said in astonishment, 'But you haven't had anything to do with the case, how can you say that?' And then she told her of our visit and ministry.

Now, however, it seemed Cordelia was seriously ill again. Once more Lucy and I went in Matron's car a fifty-mile journey to minister to her; once more on a Sunday afternoon, once more in the absence of her doctor, but this time at her doctor's personal request.

For a little while we were asked to wait, not in a room, but in some sort of corridor. Then Cordelia was wheeled, to our surprise, from whatever ward she had been in, to us in the corridor. But what surprised us even more was the change in her whole appearance. She hardly looked the same girl. There was flesh on her face, and she was to all outward appearances decidedly better. In fact, I thought to myself, the doctor must be wrong, this girl is doing fine. Then I reminded myself that the doctor must know exactly the condition of her affected lungs, and since her invitation had brought us here, then it must have been very necessary for her to have called us in for spiritual help.

Once again we all prayed, and this time I anointed Cordelia with holy oil in the name of the Blessed Trinity. We gave thanks to God, and I ended with the Blessing. So we left; but—in spite of Dr Margaret's S O S—much more happily than on the occasion of our first visit.

Soon we heard good news. Cordelia was rapidly

improving, then she was on part privileges, then on full privileges as a convalescent. Still no talk, so far as we knew, of any operation to remove the one lung. We continued to thank God.

Next, we heard that Cordelia was being allowed to go home to her parents for a holiday; this was wonderful news to them, to Cordelia herself, and to us of course. The weeks slipped by. With the approach of Christmas we were delighted when our Matron informed us that Cordelia's doctor would be bringing her to see the Nativity play which our Zulu nurses and child patients always put on in one of the wards each year. We looked forward to seeing both Cordelia and Dr Margaret, as well as our friend Dr Ray who came each year for the play. What a happy meeting it was! Ada was working on our staff once more and Cordelia herself was also working.

The Nativity play went very well, though I must admit I thought a strapping Zulu nurse dressed as one of the guardian angels round the crib looked a bit odd as she wore thick horn-rimmed spectacles—not that it mattered, of course!

There were other visitors too, plus the eighty children in our care. What did take us all by surprise was something that occurred at the very end of the play. The crib had been in the centre of the stage for about an hour, and suddenly in the last moments of the play a tiny brown-skinned arm was raised from the straw in the crib, and tiny fingers opened and shut to prove that they belonged to a real live African baby lying in the manger! Until that moment the whole audience had surmised it was a lifeless brown doll, but in fact it was the two-week-old babe of our African head boy and his wife. No producer could ever have timed such a perfect climax to a Nativity play, as the long-drawn-out 'Aaaaaa . . . h' of the delighted audience showed. True, it was a baby *girl*— but I don't think the Lord minded, and we certainly didn't. Indeed, *she* stole the show.

After leaving the hospital ward, I walked with Dr

Margaret across the grass to her waiting car. Ahead of us were an exultant Ada, another African nurse they had brought with them to see the play, Lucy, and Cordelia herself, who was so nicely dressed, and simply radiating a quiet healthful joy.

It was the first time I had had an opportunity to talk with her doctor, for we had not met till that day. I longed to hear from Dr Margaret's own lips what she thought about the healing, but somehow I felt embarrassed. We had almost reached the car, and then I screwed up my courage and said: 'Tell me, Doctor, to what do you attribute Cordelia's wonderful recovery; how do you account for it?' She stopped at once in her tracks, looked at me as though astonished that I should ask such a question, and said: 'But surely, you *must* know! We had done *every possible thing* we could, tried every single thing we knew, and to no avail. There was nothing more that could be done. This was a clear case of divine healing. It was God who healed her.'

I was satisfied. It was Jesus who said, 'It is my Father who doeth the works.'

From time to time I show slides of South Africa on my projector: one is of a happy, smiling group, which I took immediately after the Nativity play. I see again Dr Margaret, Ada and Cordelia standing beside the doctor's car and I think back to the words of Jesus who said, 'I give you power and authority to cure diseases.' In Cordelia's case He proved it. To Him be all the glory!

# 7 HOWARD AND JOHN

It was something of an occasion, for it was the first time in the history of this parish church that a healing service had been held. Four o'clock in the afternoon of a week-day may not have suited everybody who would like to have been present, but even so there was a congregation of about fifty, which was an encouragement to the vicar, and to the ladies who had formed a prayer group. They had been praying for the sick for a considerable time: behind the scenes their praying had laid the foundation for God's loving purposes.

The vicar took the service and then I preached the word, after which I moved into the sanctuary to lay hands on any who came forward for healing. The vicar had encouraged those intending to come for ministry to fill in a card with brief particulars and the name of the one to be prayed for; this would cut out the need for whispered conversation between myself and the suppliants.

As I was a complete stranger I knew nothing of those who now knelt at the altar rail for prayer. Some who came were also unknown to the vicar, but they had read the notice on the church board facing the road, or maybe a hand-done small poster in some shop, and had been moved to attend this advertised service.

One such person was a man whose name and story

were brought to memory long after the service took place. I cannot recall his features, but distinctly remember him being there, and even the exact place where he knelt amid the row of kneeling figures. He was, at a guess, in his late sixties.

The vicar stood behind him and held up a card for me to read. In large capitals it was headed: URGENT: BY PROXY. Beneath was a request for the man's son John, who was critically ill in a Johannesburg hospital hundreds of miles away. Leaning forward I read that Howard, the father who knelt before me, was also in need of prayer as he had several physical ailments. So I laid hands on him, and prayed for them both 'as the Spirit gave me utterance': then passed to the next person.

When the service was over I stood outside the church porch in the brilliant African sunshine, the congregation filing past with a word of thanks or farewell: I don't think I had any conversation with Howard, or indeed with anyone at all. What I do recall was a conversation with the wife of the churchwarden who was putting the hymn books away. She came forward, smiling happily, and said: 'I've had a healing too!', by which I thought she meant at some service a while ago. When I asked where, and when, she said, 'Here, this afternoon!' Her husband joined us at that point, looking extremely pleased, as well he might.

I gathered she had had a bad fall a few days before, had hurt her shoulder, and the pain had been sufficient to keep her awake at night. She said: 'I haven't been able to lift my arm more than a few inches.' Her husband added, 'Yes, and I've had to pour out the tea, as she couldn't even lift her arm to do that much.'

'And now?' I queried. Beaming, she raised her arm up and down quite a few times in rapid succession, obviously with no pain or difficulty. 'Looks like a lot of "Heil Hitlers" to me,' I said. At which we all had a laugh, for she could now raise the arm right up. She was one of those who had faithfully prayed for God's blessing on this service, and 'according to her faith she had received'. They became our good friends from that day; and several years later as Lucy and I were ascending an escalator at Waterloo station in London, we spied them going down the opposite one! God's timing is perfect. How our tongues wagged when they rejoined us at the top.

We made another good friend during our stay in Natal. Dora was one of those women who really enthused about divine healing. I doubt if she ever missed an opportunity to testify to the fact of Jesus healing people today by supernatural grace. Sometimes she came with our other city friends to the Healing Home, and she was always thrilled to hear stories of divine healings.

Now it so happened that two incumbents of city churches had kindly invited me to conduct a healing service bi-monthly in their respective Lady Chapels. This meant I always took a healing service monthly in the city, though numbers could not be large, as most people worked of an afternoon when these services took place.

On one occasion Dora walked in with a friend just before the service began. She introduced us, and said her friend's husband was in a nearby hospital, and due for an operation just as we were about to start our service. He had already had a colostomy performed, and the surgeon had told the wife that this second operation would be a tricky matter because of it. Once again, God's timing was perfect, and we simply began our service by holding up Tom for healing, bringing him by faith into the presence of God through silent prayer; we prayed also for the team at work in the operating theatre, especially the surgeon.

The result of this operation, a difficult one, was so successful that the case made medical history; it was reported in the *Medical Journal* because it had enabled Tom's body to function in a specific way quicker than had ever been known before. We felt we had played a small but important part in that result, for the surgeon himself told Tom's wife it was 'simply amazing the way everything went exactly right' with the operation. About forty people had shared in that 'group ministry', and all were aware of the power of prayer to bring glory to God.

About a week later I visited Tom in hospital, by which time he was getting on well. He was cheerful, and grateful for our prayers. Before leaving him, I prayed for him. Later, his wife said he had come home 'a changed man' —whatever that meant—and she used to give me the credit for it, which was quite unmerited; but it reminds us that divine healing is concerned with more than parts, or even the whole, of our physical anatomy.

It was some time later that Dora went to stay with Tom and his wife down the coast. While she was holidaying with them, an old friend of Tom came to see him. They had both lived and worked in the great city of Johannesburg and both had now retired to more beautiful and peaceful surroundings. Tom's friend had his son with him, a man in his thirties, and Dora was introduced to father and son—Howard, and John!

They chatted about Tom's improved health, of course, and soon Dora came into the conversation and spoke of the prayer behind his healing. My guess is that she then launched out into the sea of her pet subject, divine healing; I know for a fact she told them several stories of healings that had taken place in my own ministry, though didn't mention my name.

After a while Howard said : 'Oh ! my son and I believe in divine healing, and in the power of prayer. We can tell you a good story, too, if you'd like to hear it.' Dora assured them there was nothing she'd like better; whereupon Howard told of how he had retired to a house on the south coast, not all that far from where Tom was living—and, incidentally, some ten miles from the church where I had actually ministered to him. He said John had suffered a great deal from kidney trouble, and he himself had had a patch of ill health. About a year previously, his doctor was troubled about a clot of blood, and was also treating him for an angina condition of the heart. Then he had a dose of flu, and pneumonia set in. His temperature soared to 104 degrees.

'That morning,' said Howard, 'they rang through from Johannesburg about John. He had spent the past three months under specialists in a large hospital, but in vain. Renal failure had set in, and John was already unconscious. They regretted there was nothing more they could do. John could not be expected to live more than two or three days.'

One can imagine how he must have felt, lying there somewhat helplessly, and his son 430 miles away. There was nothing he could do, but pray. Then he suddenly recalled reading about a service of divine healing; moreover, it was to be that very afternoon. Again, God's timing was exactly right.

Howard had a housekeeper to care for him, and she was naturally worried about his condition, and saddened to hear about his dying son. Nevertheless, she was startled that afternoon to hear Howard descending the stairs, and she came into the hall to find him fully dressed.

'What in the world are you doing?' she asked.

'I'm going to a church down the coast,' said Howard. 'There's to be a service of healing at four o'clock.'

'Service of healing!' she echoed, 'you must be mad. You're more likely to commit suicide than get healed, going out with a temperature of 104 degrees.'

Howard replied: 'But I'm not going for myself, I'm going for my son.'

So he got the car out and drove to the church, filled in the card, heading it: 'URGENT: BY PROXY', and went up for ministry.

He told them how the minister put his hands on his head, but nothing happened. 'Then,' said Howard, 'he began to pray. And at that moment it was as if a flame of fire passed through me, from my head to my feet, filling every part of me. I can't explain, but it was what you might call a spiritual experience. It lasted for the space of half an hour.'

He paused, thinking back to that occasion. Then he continued as they listened intently to the end. 'Just at that time John regained consciousness; to their surprise, I guess! Seventeen days later he actually walked out of that hospital ward, and his kidneys were whole. The doctors couldn't understand it. Just another miracle. But I wrote to the sister in charge of the ward and asked her to make inquiries as to the exact moment, as far as possible, when John woke up. She did, and wrote to say she couldn't, of course, give the time to the minute, but she was certain he had regained consciousness within the space of a specified half-hour. And the half-hour she gave was just that in which I had that strange experience. And here we are, both of us,' Howard concluded, 'to tell the tale.'

It was then that Dora, doubtless moved by this unusual story of a double healing—for Howard was also healed—asked who it was that ministered to him. Howard said he hadn't known me, of course, but gave my surname—no mistaking that one! Whereupon Dora cried, 'But that's the man I've been talking about; he and his wife are friends of mine! Did you write and tell him?'

Howard said he had tried to, but had failed to find me, for the address given him had proved incorrect. At which Dora said: 'If you'll write him a letter and post it to me, I'll see he gets it, for he's coming to take a Mission at our church soon.'

John chimed in: 'I'd like to write to him too, and thank him for his part in my healing.'

Thus it was that at a time when we were feeling much in need of uplift ourselves, I was handed the letters they had written me, and addressed to Dora's home. About to begin, so far as Lucy and I were concerned, our last 'healing venture' in Natal, those letters really lifted our hearts with praise to God, who once again had timed things perfectly.

An interesting thing was that Howard said the healings took place on Kruger's Day, which is an important day to South Africans; and the morning we read their letters was also Kruger's Day, exactly one year after God had touched both father and son at the same time, though they were hundreds of miles apart. But, of course, neither time nor distance can set a limit to His own gracious purposes of power and love.

## 8  LEAH

In addition to the resident patients at the Healing Home
in Natal, we often took visitors for short periods. They
came for needful rest and recuperation, to get away
from the stresses and strains of life, and sometimes because they were physically ill. Others came for a holiday
in quiet and beautiful surroundings, bringing with them
their own problems which were sometimes solved while
they were with us, after prayer and counsel. Some came
more than a thousand miles for help; and one woman
came to us all the way from England—some six thousand
miles!—while many more came hundreds of miles or
less, because we practised this ministry of divine healing; all of which goes to prove both the demand for it,
and the sad fact of a dearth of such Homes as ours.

From the point of view of the staff, though visitors
added to our work, they also brought us a much needed
change of company and conversation; for we lived in a
quiet part of the world with patients who had proved too
difficult to be kept in their own homes. There were, of
course, resident patients who were not of that category,
some of whom expected to stay at the Home till they
ended their days.

Leah was one of those who came for a short stay, only
three weeks, but she had a problem which had really
got her down. Her letter of inquiry as to whether we took
visitors for only a short period was written in a poor

hand, the lines not being straight, and the words something of a squiggle.

She was able to have one of the private rooms in what is called The Sanctuary; the magnificent view from it was of a wide expanse of green, over gently undulating hills, beyond which could be glimpsed the blue of the ocean. The still loveliness must have brought rest to many a troubled soul who would sit in the garden; and here visitors would often share confidences with each other to their mutual satisfaction. The sunshine, the peace, the surrounding beauty of the place, as well as the sharing of one's troubles, all played a part in the healing of those who came.

I took stock of Leah as she moved slowly with the aid of a stick across the visitors' dining room to a place allocated to her at one of the small tables. She was above average height, well built, and her white hair piled high upon her head made her look rather distinguished and taller than she actually was. She wore glasses unlike any I had ever seen before, one lens being completely frosted over, the other similarly, but for a small, plain centrepiece which 'tunnelled' her vision that was quite obviously very limited. She bent low over her plate as she stabbed at her food with a fork, but in addition to that, the stoop of her shoulders betokened a burden she found grievous to bear.

We discovered she was quite a talker, but soon learned that her husband was a quiet man; and as their family had married and gone elsewhere to live, except for one daughter who lived near her parents and was now looking after her father while her mother stayed with us, Leah hadn't much in the way of an audience at home! However, she was a motherly soul, and in a day or two everyone decided they liked her and felt sorry for her.

She was, in fact, Afrikaans, and had always worked hard because her husband was a sugar farmer. Like many of her people she had deep religious convictions, but, unfortunately, her husband had none. His complete lack of sensitivity to the love of God, his utter disinterest in things spiritual, had created a division between them that may well have first begun years before when he refused even to attend the baptisms of his own children. I wondered whether this very real sorrow in her mind and heart was responsible for the arthritis which now made her walking difficult and slow.

Reminiscing, Leah told me her husband had toiled on the farm all his married life, and had done well enough to provide for them and their children both necessities and luxuries. Now he was getting old, and had nothing to look forward to. True, he could look back over the years, recall the good seasons and the bad, and take some pride in his achievements. But what of the future? He was often ill, and this had taken toll of her own physical strength as she had had to nurse him. With nothing to comfort him by way of Christian faith, no wonder he had become more difficult to live with. What she found most trying was his hardness and lack of appreciation of her; never once did he think to say 'thank you' for any service she rendered.

St Paul sums up the truth of such living in his letter to the Galatians: 'Be not deceived; God is not mocked: for whatsoever a man soweth, that shall he also reap. For he that soweth to his flesh shall of the flesh reap corruption; but he that soweth to the Spirit shall of the Spirit reap life everlasting.' This is not to say his children did not love him; indeed, they loved both their parents.

Leah said she would sometimes talk to him about their children and grandchildren. She would say: 'Now that we are old we should be telling them how gracious God has been to us all our life; how He has provided all good things for us and for them. We should be pointing out to them the lessons we have learnt, and show them that life is more than money and the things it can buy, good though the things may be. We should be telling them that some day, they too must go on from this life to the next, and should live according to His way.'

Maybe her words only irked him the more, as is not uncommon in such cases. He did not change, nor indeed, could he of himself, for this was a bondage of the enemy. Nothing mars a personal relationship more decisively than a lack of love, and that hardness of heart which comes to those who leave God out of account in their lives, or who have wrong ideas of God.

Our greatest friends in Natal, to whom we are ever grateful for their love toward us, and without whose kindness and help our lives at times would have been decidedly bleak, are a married couple; he is English, she is Afrikaans. We did not meet very many Afrikaans people, but like all people they vary. Each nation has its own characteristics, the reserve of the English, for example, but there are always plenty of exceptions to the rule. At the end of a little more than two years in a country one can only have but an idea of a people, and mine might have been unfair to the Afrikaans. But I felt from what I had heard, seen and read that Leah's husband might have been a true son of the tough *voortrekkers*.

It was at the end of our stay that I put a question to an Afrikaans *domine* (pastor). I told him I had formed an opinion which could be utterly wrong, but wondered if he would agree that many of his people speak, feel and act as they do because they still retain, by and large, an Old Testament idea of God, rather than the image of God which the loving Jesus sets before us. I wasn't being rude or unkind—I really wanted to know, and, in fact, had an admiration for this sincere and intellectual man of God.

After voicing my question, he bowed his head, and he was so long without speaking or looking up that I hoped I hadn't hurt his feelings. When he did look up he said very sadly, 'Yes, you are quite right.' Maybe this explains many things in that beautiful country which are difficult for other Christians to understand. True, we are not here to condemn, not if we follow Christ, but no matter what our nationality, it is for all Christians to witness to God as one who is infinite Love, and who walked this earth once as man, and that in the person of His Son, Jesus.

Leah had reached a point where she desperately needed a 'break', a holiday and a rest; frustration and a deep sense of hurt utterly oppressed her. To give him his due, her husband saw her need, and wanted her to go to one or other of their distant married children; and she had friends scattered in other places who would have welcomed her as gladly as her family. At the end of her stay with us Leah told me how she thought and talked of this and that alternative, till finally she was in a state of complete indecision.

It was her custom to sit in her chair beside her bed last thing at night and read her Bible. One night, having done so, she suddenly went on her knees beside her bed and cried to God to tell her what to do and where to go. She slept well that night, and just before waking it was as if someone was calling her by name: 'Leah . . . Leah . . . Leah! You are very tired, and you need a holiday, a good rest. But you don't know where to go. So many places to choose from, so many friends who would gladly have you. Well, go to . . .' (mentioning the name of our Healing Home) 'and there you will find the answer to your needs.' She awoke instantly, and it was as if the room still echoed with the words. She sat up and took the pencil and notebook which she always kept beside her bed, not least to jot things down after her Bible reading and prayer, for her memory sometimes played her tricks; how wise of her! When God speaks, it is good to write our thoughts down, or we tend to forget them, and disappoint or disobey Him.

Having written the name of our Home—which was to her no more than a name—she got up and dressed herself, trembling with excitement. God had surely sent an angel to tell her where to go.

Of course she daren't tell her husband, he'd think her

75

mad . . . so she didn't! But when he had left the house after breakfast she wrote her scrawly lines to me to ask if we took short stay visitors. Not long afterwards, she joined us at the Home.

On the Sunday she climbed a series of terraced steps from her room to the chapel for the regular weekly healing service. She sat in one of the front row armed chairs reserved for those who could not kneel for the laying on of hands, those who were too stiff or crippled, and the blind; I always ministered to such people first. The service proceeded as usual, the word was preached —and when it is we have a right to expect signs to follow. I ministered to Leah as to the others, and noticed she kept her eyes shut a long time after I had prayed.

The service over, we followed the bell's call to lunch, but I didn't notice that Leah was absent from her place; I think other day visitors kept my attention. In the afternoon I went off to preach in a parish many miles distant, so did not see Leah until next morning.

After grace, we sat down to breakfast, but Leah beckoned me, so, rising, I went to her table. I could see she was very perturbed about something, and asked what she wanted; she was trembling, and was so moved that one or two tears ran down her cheeks. My heart sank: 'Has someone upset you?' I asked. For sometimes patients did upset other people. 'No!' she replied, brushing the tears away, 'I just want to tell you something after breakfast.'

'Why not now?' I asked, thinking I might put the matter right straight away. She smiled: 'Well! I wanted to tell you I had a healing at the service yesterday.' It was a relief to know her tears were tears of joy. 'Well, that's wonderful!' I said, 'and what a lovely beginning to a Monday morning! That's something to rejoice over . . . but tell me afterwards all about it.' And so she did.

It was all so quiet and simple . . . what He did! As I

prayed it seems her whole body was strangely filled with a wondrous light . . . 'every part of it, through and through', was the way she described it.

'After the service,' she said, 'I didn't want any lunch —only to get to my room and sit quietly, and enjoy the healing. On the way down the steps I met Sister M who was coming up with an enamel bowl and some bandages in her hands. As she passed me I just fell on her and embraced her, saying "O, Sister!"—I just couldn't help it!' Now that particular nursing sister was a fine Christian, but hardly the one to fall upon in an embrace! Moreover, she was rather small and by no means young, and the picture of Leah majestically overwhelming her is not easily forgotten. Sister told me later she thought Leah was having a heart attack, and was frightened by her for the moment. Then she learned Leah had had a healing touch from the Lord. True to form, that evening Sister visited Leah for prayer and thanksgiving, and left her some tracts.

And what kind of a healing was it? True, she never again needed her stick to walk on our stony paths; and her sight was so much improved that she was surprised next day to find the chapel carpet was not of one colour, but of various colours and patterns which she hadn't discerned before. But the best part of her healing was the infilling of light she received. Light drives away the darkness: and Leah was no longer in darkness as she had been. Jesus said He is the Light of the World, and we, as His disciples, are to be as lights to others.

From the moment of His touch upon her, Leah was renewed in every way. Everyone could see the change in her, the joy and the love which reached out to touch others.

I recall that a day or two later in the dining room she was asked to change tables as another guest had ended her stay and left. Leah now came to sit at a table opposite our own. Looking across, I remembered how jaded she had looked the first night she came and sat at table, how she bent low to see the food on her plate; to say nothing of the stoop of her shoulders.

At an appropriate moment I nudged Lucy, and nodded in Leah's direction. We both had a laugh, we couldn't help it, for the transformation in her was a joy to see. Leah was sitting absolutely upright, like 'la grande dame', no bending low to stab—of all things on this occasion—sweetcorn! She raised her loaded fork un-erringly and with complete success, her sight giving her no trouble: who could have thought she had ever stooped in her life!

One day, about a week later, I saw a lovely car on the drive, and then noticed Leah standing at the other side of it. I had forgotten the daughter was bringing her father to find out how her mother was faring. As I crossed the drive, a very smart young woman at the wheel looked across at me, and guessed who I was. In clear and haughty tones, much to my surprise, she called out: 'Mr Jeremiah! What *have* you been doing to my mother?' I was quite taken aback: 'Why?' I stammered . . . 'I don't know what you mean.' Then her face changed, and laughing happily she exclaimed, 'Well, my mother looks at least TWENTY years younger! I don't know how you did it, but I think I'll have to come and stay here myself, and see what happens!'

So I met Leah's husband and daughter, just briefly. As for Leah, the burden had been lifted, she herself was full of the joy of the Lord, and there is no joy to equal that. True, she had to return home to the same situation, but, changed by the power of our Loving God, she could now cope. Indeed, several weeks later she wrote to me, thank-ing everyone for all they had done for her. In her letter, no longer a squiggly affair, as she once termed it, she wrote frankly: 'I look back with longing to the Home and all the dear people I met. I thank you all from my heart for everything. Of course my husband is just the same, but that doesn't matter in the way it used to, for I still have the Light within me, and I know it will never leave me, no matter what happens.' She might have been more accurate to say 'He' rather than 'it'; for Jesus is the light that lighteth everyone that cometh into the world. Yet it is only to 'as many as receive Him' that He says : 'I will never leave thee, nor forsake thee.'

# 9  THE CHILDREN

The Gospels clearly portray the love of Jesus for children. On one occasion we read of mothers bringing their little ones to Him for a blessing, maybe for His healing touch. They would not have done so if He had been a stern-faced rabbi intolerant of their offspring. They knew His infectious joy, and no one told stories better than He, while the children themselves clearly trusted Him, and children are quick to respond to love. In the home at Nazareth He may well have had responsibility for half a dozen younger brothers and sisters after the death of Joseph, His foster-father.

In an age when children were kept in their place, it was natural enough for the twelve disciples to turn the mothers and their children away from their Master, who was a very busy man. It came as something of a shock when He rebuked them, saying: 'Let the children come unto me, for of such is the kingdom of heaven.' That must have been something of a puzzle to them, but then the Master often said things that held a deeper meaning, and He didn't always explain either.

On another occasion these same disciples were arguing as to their own importance. Jesus then took a little boy and set him in their midst, using him as an object lesson, saying: 'Whosoever shall receive one of such children in my name receives me: and whosoever receives me, receives not me, but Him that sent Me.' This

He said after another strange word: 'If any man desire to be first, the same shall be last of all, and servant of all.'

The picture of Jesus taking the child in His arms was one that lingered long in the memory of the disciples, but they had yet to learn the great value God sets upon children. They were adults, but immature, as adults often are. That we receive God when we receive a child is a sobering thought. Sterner still was the warning Jesus gave to any who would grievously harm children: 'Whosoever shall offend one of these little ones that believe in me, it were better for him that a millstone were hanged about his neck, and he were cast into the sea.'

One of the joys of my having received a ministry of healing was to minister at times to every Zulu child in our care at the hospital on our estate. To go amongst them at other times was also a pleasure to me, and they always gave one a great welcome even though there was a language barrier between some of us. Older ones, however, would interpret the little rhymes or songs I would teach them out of school hours, the little ones quick enough to get the fun of them. There were, among these TB convalescents, sometimes other ailments, but from time to time we knew that prayer brought healing. Almost all the staff members, Africans, also received the laying on of hands with prayer when the ministry was to all children at a special healing service; these we held several times a year.

Yet it was when I went outside the Healing Home to other places that I was given unexpected opportunities to minister to children, and the colour of their skin proved no barrier to the healing touch of Jesus. Sometimes it was a private visit to a European home, or again, to a church service where children walked or were carried to the sanctuary rail to be prayed for in the name of Jesus. Occasionally, an African mother would kneel while I prayed for her and the baby suckling at her breast; somewhat unusual, but so natural. In every case I believe a blessing was bestowed, and sometimes a healing.

For the encouragement of parents and others concerned for sick children, I recount some of the things that happened in Natal.

## Angeline

It was from Angeline's father that I received a letter telling me of her need, and how the Lord had met it. During a visit to a south-coast Anglican church at which the Africans were made welcome, I ministered to this five-year-old girl whose parents were Christians. They regularly attended an Assemblies of God church where the ministry of divine healing was taught and practised. What medical history may have been behind the child's need I don't know, but the father had heard of a healing service to be held at this Anglican church and brought his daughter to be ministered to.

She was paralysed down one side of her body, and in consequence could not walk or run around at play like other children. One side of her face was affected so that jaw movement was difficult, and this made her unable to speak or chew solid food. What must her life have been like? How earnestly must her parents have prayed.

Angeline's father carried her back to the pew, and possibly a good many miles to their home, but the carrying days were now limited. His letter, written a month or more later, told of their joy, for Angeline was almost completely free of paralysis. She was able to walk and run around with her playmates, and her jaw was working normally so that she could now sing little hymns they had taught her, and eat solid food. I did not meet them again, but the honesty of the letter was apparent.

Firstly, her father said, 'She is free from paralysis except that she is not quite able to grip things properly with her hand, but the devil is well on the way out and will soon be gone completely!' That was his way of looking at it.

The other thing was that he enclosed a gift for 1 Rand (fifty pence) for the Healing Home's work. This was no mean gift, for the wage of an African was not to be compared with that of his European counterpart. In itself the gift was a testimony to the healing work of Jesus. He ended his letter with a word of praise: 'Hallelujah!' We certainly echoed it.

### Sindisi

On two occasions when the time came for our holiday we gladly accepted a kind invitation to stay in a church-owned house on the south coast; it was actually next door to the church where Angeline, and others, received healing: whenever I ministered there with the vicar, we always heard of people who had received a blessing. Perhaps it was this which endeared us to each other there, for we made many friends. The pleasant house was what we would call a bungalow, but I recall the shock someone expressed when I thanked them for the use of the bungalow; it seems in Natal a bungalow is a mere beach-hut! I hastily apologised, for we loved to be in it in privacy, yet only two hundred yards from an attractive beach. We could glimpse from the front windows the great breakers of the Indian Ocean as they flung pebbles and shingle with great force on the shore; not a place to swim in, but we could lie on the edge and get peppered with stinging shale and, after the heat of the sun, what seemed like ice-cold sea water. This was great fun, and how essential to get away from the Healing Home where the enemy was busier than I had ever known him in my life.

I recall the greeting I had on returning home from one of these holidays. A woman met me at the main door saying, 'Thank God you're back, Warden. It's been hell here while you've been away!' Alas, it sometimes was; but wherever you find Divine Healing being practised, especially in a community, I think it almost inevitable that the enemy whom Christ knew in His day will be active in ours to a degree of subtlety and evil that we do not experience in the ordinary run of Christian living. The devil hates men to know that Christ heals today; that lesson I learned in South Africa.

It was on the last day of our second holiday that we were destined to meet a beautiful brown-skinned African baby girl named Sindisi. Having packed our luggage, we went to the nearby town to do some last-minute shopping. Lucy returned a little before me, and our African house-girl told her we had callers. She beckoned to her and pointed through the back windows. Lucy saw something strangely moving, for on the small lawn were three figures; one, an African grannie, as she proved to be; another, a girl of some twelve years who was her granddaughter—they were both kneeling there and praying aloud, the grannie, arms uplifted, storming the gates of Heaven in voluble prayer, the girl likewise but not so noisily. Between them, lying prone and silent, was Sindisi, the girl's baby sister. Sindisi should be walking, but could only lie flat.

Shortly afterwards I returned. Our time was short, for we were to motor about 140 miles home immediately after lunch. Lucy had gathered by now that Grannie had been a faithful attender at the Sunday afternoon services; had heard me tell of Jesus as Divine Healer. One of her daughters, the mother of Sindisi, worked in the home of a European doctor. There was something wrong with Sindisi's hips, or legs—exactly what I wouldn't know. Consequently, the doctor took a professional interest in her, and she had been most carefully examined by a surgeon. His verdict was that they could do nothing to enable her to walk for another three years, when there could be surgery, though at this stage he could not promise it would be successful. Grannie had witnessed to Sindisi's mother, and now had brought her child for healing prayer.

The child was spotlessly clean, content to lie still in the hot sunshine, and she wore a beautiful dress which, I imagined, was a gift from the doctor's wife. But babes are not meant to lie flat on their backs for years, unable to sit or stand or walk. How helpless in the natural one feels at such a time. The girl had carried the babe, who was quite some weight though I couldn't guess as to her age, some four miles to be prayed for; she looked at me solemnly in silence. The grannie had faith, you could see it in her eyes; Lucy had seen it through the window when Grannie, with arms uplifted as she knelt and prayed aloud, had called upon God for a miracle. Do we not find in the Gospel that same faith of childlike quality that Jesus Himself commends? When doctors and ministers of the gospel are helpless, both may turn to Him, who made our bodies to work according to His loving purposes, in prayer.

We called our house-girl to come out and join us. So we all knelt together on the grass; Lucy and I placed our hands upon this needy child, and I prayed.

Lucy then hurried indoors, asking Grannie to wait a moment. She soon returned and handed her a stamped addressed envelope, saying: 'I happened to have this in my handbag, so I've addressed it to my husband . . . everything else is packed! When Sindisi starts to walk, please write a few lines and post the letter to us at the Healing Home.' With broad smiles Grannie thanked us, and the trio began their journey back to the African location from whence they had come.

We soon forgot about Sindisi, though her name may well have gone out to our intercessors. One day at the Home a couple of months later, when sorting the incoming mail, I saw an envelope addressed to me in what was obviously Lucy's hand. It seemed odd, since she was at the Home with me. I'd forgotten all about it. Opening it, I read Grannie's nicely penned note. She began by expressing the hope that we were well, went on to talk about the weather, finally ending with a note of triumph : '. . . and I am writing this to tell you that Sindisi has *already* started to walk'. How wonderful, His touch!

There would be no need to wait for three years, no need for any operation. We had not known as we prayed for Sindisi that those minutes were to be a fitting climax to our last visit to that parish, but at the end of the year we sailed back home. When our friends read this they will know how their prayers for us and our ministry in and around their church were really answered up to our last moments in their midst. Moreover, the Lord received added glory through another miracle of His grace towards a helpless child.

## Percival and Livingstone

Not many of the Anglican clergy I met showed much interest in the subject of the Church's ministry of Divine Healing. However, in view of the fact that I had had little interest in, and almost no knowledge of it myself until recent months, I could hardly be critical of them. There were a few European priests who invited me to preach about the work of the Healing Home, others who were glad to hold a healing service, and even occasionally a week's mission in a parish. These visits were blessed at the time, and one always prayed that good seed would bring forth more fruit eventually. Yet there were days when I longed to tell more people of the work of the Healing Home and of the miracles the Lord had wrought among us in the face of almost insuperable odds against which one battled at the Home itself. Nevertheless, in spite of the lack of much support from Church and State, a great deal was accomplished by a few for many needy people; the work and workers deserved greater backing. Generally speaking, however, we were by-passed, so that people who should have been stirred by the Holy Spirit to prayer and faith that would produce miracles in their own churches remained in ignorance.

Because I felt I had something to say that was worth hearing, and because healings *were* taking place, I felt frustrated by the many closed church doors. I wanted to proclaim what was new in my own experience: 'Jesus heals TODAY!' Maybe many clergy knew of this ministry . . . but did they practise it? . . . and if so, were they like one priest who did, and occasionally saw healings result, but said nothing about it even to his parishioners, let alone his fellow clergy. He thought he was being humble, truly so. In fact, he denied the Lord glory, and the witness He commands—not asks!—us to give. Of course we are concerned with a man's wholeness, not just physical health, but every time Jesus wrought a miracle of healing in His earthly life He *showed* the kingdom of heaven at hand. So He does today . . . when He can find His own with sufficient faith and courage to act as well as talk. The 'signs' John wrote of in his gospel to reveal the divinity of Christ are also present in our midst today. It is to His glory when we tell of them.

So it was with surprised pleasure that one day I received an invitation from an African priest. He had spiritual supervision over a vast number of Africans living in a location set apart for them by the Government some miles from the city. Would I be willing to come and talk to his congregation about Divine Healing, and minister to any in need? Would I? I jumped at the chance.

Europeans were not allowed to go into a location, of course, without the necessary official permit. This I obtained, and the appropriate date and time allowed 'in' was duly noted by officialdom. Originally, I thought to go on a Sunday, but we were strongly advised, Lucy and I, not to do so. Should we, by accident, happen to touch, let alone injure, an African on one of their crowded thoroughfares when driving in the dark, we might trigger off real trouble. Moreover, at weekends men often drowned their sorrows by taking more alcohol than was good for them. Press reports frequently spoke of violence among the Africans on Sundays; sometimes brawls ended in murder. So we settled for a weeknight service.

The vicar met us in his car at the main entrance gate and handed our permit to the African policeman on duty. We followed our guide in our car along the dimly-lit highways and byways of what seemed to me a maze of turnings. I could never have found the way without a guide.

The church, dedicated to the memory of the man who carried the Cross of Jesus to Golgotha on Good Friday, St Simon of Cyrene, was a vast brick building. For a mid-week service it was a very good congregation, all ages represented, and plenty of children, some in parental arms. The singing you cannot appreciate unless you have heard it for yourself. Even at the Home, when a few Zulu orderlies and nurses were given a note from a tuning fork, and no other music, they had only to sing a few bars to bring a lump to my throat and tears to my eyes. Now, looking down the church at perhaps the poorest congregation I had ever worshipped with, I thought of Simon of Cyrene, who may well have been as dark-skinned as these children of God. The vicar, in answer to a question I had casually put him in the vestry, had said I was the first European priest to preach in the church since the day of its actual consecration several years ago. That made me a sad but privileged person in a new way. I could but pray that Jesus would use me. Many came forward, perhaps for the first time in their lives, for such a ministry, and they were very reverent. When the service ended I went to the west door to bid them a good night.

Turning to come back down the aisle with Lucy, who

had joined me, we found a mother still sitting on her chair with a tiny scrap of humanity on her knee. The vicar joined us, and we heard the story of Livingstone. This poor little baby that looked so sickly had a great name, but we were not surprised to hear there was little hope of his survival according to medical opinion. He dribbled down his chin, his eyes wobbled uncontrollably, and one wondered if he was subnormal mentally. One thing was very clear : his mother loved him, he was precious to her, and she wanted me to pray for him. Of course I did. So ended our first visit to this church.

A matter of a few weeks later I had an open postcard from the vicar stating: 'The little boy you laid hands on and prayed for at the altar has started to walk. He could not even stand unaided before.' The simple information naturally pleased me, but roused my curiosity for I had prayed over a number of little boys, and wondered which it was  When we made a return visit I met him, also his grannie who had carried him several miles on our first visit, and since he was a fairly heavy four-year-old lad that was no light task. He boasted the name of Percival. She had even carried him home that wet night after he received laying on of hands and prayer. Putting him down, she went to see to some food, but he called her back, saying, 'Look, Grannie, I'm standing on my own!' He was, and then began walking for the first time. True, he had a way of his own of throwing out his feet as he walked, but at least he *was* walking. We came across several African children retarded that way, but this one at least became a happy little boy through our visit; and his grandmother was thrilled. So was Percival.

We also saw Livingstone again, though it would not have surprised us to hear he had left this world.

To us he still looked a poorly little babe, but his mother had brought him for more prayer, and was very sure a miracle had taken place, indeed, the medical people at the hospital had said so. Some digestive organ was missing at birth, but apparently something remarkable had happened—Livingstone could now digest food. Previously, he had spent most of his days and nights crying for food which he could not contain or digest, and was constantly hungry.

Now, he could and did eat, but he had a stricture in his bowel so that whenever he ate anything he screamed with agony when it came to passing a motion. Once again we prayed for him.

Our third and final visit to this church was marred, from my point of view, by only one thing. During my address, which had to be interpreted, a little boy was thoroughly enjoying himself pushing one of the tubular chairs backwards and forwards, and at times even across the uncarpeted nave, so that the noise he created echoed disturbingly. No one else seemed to mind, but then I was the preacher, not they; it was something of a battle for me to concentrate.

Lucy sat immediately behind the child's mother, and when service ended was surprised to find it was Livingstone's mother. Beaming with pleasure she re-introduced her all-important son. Coming down the nave I could scarcely believe it was indeed Livingstone who had been playing trains with a heavy chair. True, a year makes a difference, and it was about that length of time since we had last met, but the change was incredible. In answer to prayer the stricture had disappeared, and health had resulted. What could not fail to impress anyone was his hair. We had never seen such a crop on so young a head. Lucy could not refrain from asking about it, since it stood up as straight as a bush some four inches, if not more, all over his head. His mother, somewhat surprised at the question since to her the reason was obvious, said, 'Surely you know Samson's strength was in his hair? So we have never cut Livingstone's!' Returning home in the car it was easy to sing 'How great Thou art.'

## Vincent

Having written of the love of Africans for their children perhaps the story of Vincent is a rare exception to prove the rule : I hope so.

Matron rang me from the hospital saying she was very busy, but would I please go at once and baptise a tiny baby who had been sent from a not-far-distant general hospital to us. She added that it was not a case for us, as our children were all TB convalescents, so she had rung a city hospital and they had agreed to collect this baby shortly. Matron also said the baby was so far gone there seemed no hope of recovery, and being an Episcopalian she felt the child should be baptised.

Walking through the grounds to the nearby hospital, I wondered where the parents were, who they were, and how they could behave as they had. Apparently they had brought this baby boy to the general hospital, a nurse had taken some particulars, and the baby, but the parents disappeared, not wanting the baby at all.

When I entered a small room where two Zulu uniformed nurses were in attendance I saw the first starving child I'd ever seen in my life. As a member of the Oxfam Committee I was accustomed to see some grim photographs of such sufferers from *kwashiorkor*. To see a living victim came as a shock. Skin stretched tightly over his facial bones, he seemed to be nothing but two large dark eyes distended from their sockets. His thin little arms bore burn marks, possibly the result of deliberate application of cigarettes by his parents. Frankly, I felt angry and sickened. This in all probability was no case of a child dying from poverty, but a deliberate neglect by parents who didn't want him, who waited until he was almost dead, and then saddled a hospital with him and ran away. Only God knows.

Indeed, God did know, and I had so little that I could give that I put aside any earlier thoughts about baptising an infant without parental permission.

There was a clean napkin beside a bowl of water, but I feared to pick the tiny mite up, so puny was he. I asked the Zulu girls if they knew his name; they nodded. 'Well, what is it?' I asked. Their glance went from me to each other, and they remained silent. Maybe they, too, were upset and sickened at his condition, and ashamed of the parents whom none of us knew.

'Tell me his name,' I said again, 'that I may baptise him.' And one of the girls spoke a name which to me was the longest-sounding one I'd ever heard, or the most unpronounceable one in her Zulu tongue. This was the name given when he was handed over at the other hospital by his parents.

For some reason, knowing that Africans often have names with a meaning to them, I asked what the name meant, but it became obvious that they didn't like to tell me. I insisted, so one said, 'His name means: "Throw it out".' It sounded so apt I said, 'I cannot possibly call him by that name.' They were silent. And then I remembered it was a saint's day, one of the lesser known ones who gave his life for Christ long, long ago. 'I'll call him Vincent,' I said, 'for today is St Vincent's Day. He was a deacon and martyr for the Faith long ago.' So I baptised him and gave him that name. Shortly after I left he was collected for care in a large city hospital over fifty miles away.

It was some months later that Matron rang that hospital's matron on business, and she called this unwanted little African baby to mind, and so asked her if she knew anything of him, though she assumed he had died shortly after he left us. To our joy, we learned then that Vincent was alive and well. They had given him every medical care, and the love he so sadly needed.

I wonder sometimes what he will be in life. And whenever we sing a well-known hymn: 'Hark, my soul! it is the Lord', I recall him to mind, his simple baptism, the equally simple prayer of mine as I placed a hand upon him that morning when I asked Jesus to do for

Vincent the Father's will. Matron and I rejoiced in the expert care and attention given to that unloved baby; we, too, could sing, 'Hark, my soul! it is the Lord', but the verses that bring us truth are worth recalling :

> *Can a woman's tender care*
> *Cease towards the child she bare?*
> *Yes, she may forgetful be,*
> *Yet will I remember thee.*
>
> *Mine is an unchanging love,*
> *Higher than the heights above,*
> *Deeper than the depths beneath,*
> *Free and faithful, strong as death.*

How blest are we who had parental care—and LOVE. How rich are we who know in sickness and in health God's redeeming Love in Jesus the Saviour of mankind.

## Jason

Our promised stay of two years in Natal had ended. Our cases were packed, and we wrongly thought our ministry at the Home was ended, but not quite. Our Indian house-girl asked if, as a favour, I would pray for her nephew, Jason by name. Her family had received a number of blessings through our ministry, but of Jason I had yet to learn. She said he was seven years old, a dear little boy, but a chronic sufferer from asthma. His parents were practising Christians, but lived more than twenty miles away.

'Really!' I chided. 'We have only a day left. Why didn't you ask before?'

Well, only she knew the answer to that, and I said if they brought him I would pray for his healing. Happily, she was able to contact them by phone, and they came.

The parents had known many days and nights of anguish through the suffering of their young son. He proved to be a delightfully smiling child, though a little shy, as Asiatics often are. He had been taught about Jesus, of course, and prayed his simple prayers as children do. The years had given him much suffering, and because of the condition over the years he was what I would have called pigeon-chested, as one sees in such cases at times.

I talked to them of Jesus as Healer, of His love for boys and girls, but said we must all believe. We were just going to ask Jesus to take away whatever caused the breathlessness, and to heal every part of his chest.

After my short prayer, and thanks from the parents, they went their way. Next day we went ours, back to our own loved ones thousands of miles away. Not surprisingly, I forgot about their visit. Three years passed, and then we received a letter from Jason's aunt. In it she said, 'Jason never had a sign of asthma from the day you prayed for him, over three years ago. But this Christmas he had a slight attack. Please write and tell us what to do.'

So, after all, our last moments at the Home had been blessed by Him who called us there, and called us home at the end of our promised stay. I wrote and told them to do what I had done. To lay hands on the boy and rebuke the enemy in the name of Jesus, to pray for his complete healing in the name of Jesus in real faith. What else could one say? His Word is: 'To as many as believe . . . they shall lay hands on the sick, and they shall recover.'

Let the conditions be right, the faith strong, and let us claim His promise. Indeed, it is the children at times who have what we adults lack; no wonder Jesus often answers their simple prayers.

## 10 JANE

It was early summer in London and the beauty of the blossoming trees outside the London Healing Mission warmed the hearts of those who had eyes to see, even as the pleasant sunshine warmed the limbs of passers-by as they went about their business. It was just fifty days since I had become a member of the Mission staff. Lucy and I were living on the premises, and the process of settling once more into new surroundings was accomplished. But I longed to have more to do, and, let it be said, for exciting results in my ministry. The snare of success is ever apt to catch the Christian who wants to see results, who tends to judge his usefulness to God and man alike by dramatic happenings, who has in fact his eyes upon himself rather than his Maker. There is always the danger to the spiritually immature that success may become an end in itself, whereas in God's sight what matters most is our simple obedience to His revealed will.

We had originally promised to stay two years in Natal, after which we would seek the leading of the Holy Spirit as to the future; for not only are we meant to be *what* He would have us be, but to be *where* He would have us be. At the end of that period we were clearly led home, and, after a time of waiting on Him, to the London Healing Mission.

During the homeward voyage we often wondered

where we would eventually go, and looking back, we gratefully remembered many healings the Lord had done during our stay in South Africa. Yet I recall doubts at that time about my ministry, not least because we found the simple African folk received healing more easily than Europeans, as if those given a good education were at a disadvantage, lacking a more childlike faith. Only time could tell whether He would use me in my own country.

Now, back in London, I was itching to be on the go, longing to be used of Him to bring healing to those who suffered, and His peace to troubled souls. Maybe the warm sunshine on that particular afternoon helped to turn my thoughts to Africa, and nostalgic memories crowded in. The shrill call of the telephone brought me back to the present. From the ensuing conversation with a troubled mother about her daughter Jane, I became involved with a family I had not met, and in time we became friends. The very next afternoon I called on them and ministered to Jane, who was in her early thirties, and she gave me additional facts to those her mother had given to complete the picture.

It seemed that the trouble really began some eight years before when Jane was driving her car, and a careless driver ran into the back of her car forcefully enough to cause serious injury to her neck and the top of her spine. She received from the sudden impact what is called a 'whiplash'. Resulting from this was a stay of a year and three months in hospital, for it was one of those injuries which the best of surgeons can do little about. I actually saw x-rays taken some four years ago, that is four years after the accident, and three of the vertebrae seemed to be hooked together; she explained that the dark patches were atrophied muscles which had received no life-giving blood for the past eight years, and had ceased to serve any useful purpose. As she put it herself : 'I have lived with pain for eight years, but one gets used to it. I had the best of treatment and care available in two hospitals during those fifteen months, but at the end of it I only had some twenty to fifty per cent neck movement in various directions.'

For some years now her work as a radiographer in a busy hospital had enabled her to learn a great deal about the problems that arise concerning head, neck and spinal injuries. This was of little comfort to her the day I called, for she had most unfortunately been involved in another accident: she knew her own case. Sitting in the front of a friend's car as a passenger while her friend was driving, they came to a crossroad where a car travelling at high speed across their path swerved, missed them by inches, and careered on. Her friend braked suddenly, and if they had not been strapped in they might well have gone through the windscreen; as it was, the sudden braking jarred Jane so much that it brought about a replica of her first accident. She slept little that night, not only because of all the old symptoms and the pain they produced, but also because of the doubts and fears as to her future. She courageously went to work next day, but whilst working, the surgeon spotted her need. Forthwith she was sent home and ordered to lie flat on her back wearing a high plastic collar; it was hoped that by lying as still as possible, the neck would in time right itself.

Her mother looked after her and shared her concern, and three weeks passed. Then came an unforgettable night. Endeavouring to help Jane after a bath, she dropped a towel round Jane's shoulders and seemingly did something to the vertebrae. So intense was the pain that her mother gave her as much sedation as she thought she dared, Jane herself not wishing to disturb the surgeon who would have left the hospital anyway; and knowing there was little to be done for her without risking paralysis or even her life, she decided to put up with it. For the next four hours her mother shared in the agony, watching Jane's head slowly but surely bending and moving inexorably round until it was almost under her arm and, even more frightening, facing back to front like the head of a celluloid doll. Finally, her mother, fearing the worst, rang the surgeon and on his advice gave more sedation. From then on her head slowly began to return to its normal position.

The following day, knowing and appreciating the dilemma of medical men at the top of their profession, Jane's mother rang up various people who might be able and willing to help as they had experience in the Church's ministry of healing. She drew blank or negative response, and finally rang the London Healing Mission. After hearing from her the need, I agreed to visit them the next afternoon, but before she rang off she made me promise not to actually lay hands on Jane's head, as she simply could not stand the slightest touch for the pain it would incur.

Next morning, in my early quiet time, I felt positive I was directed to lay my hands on Jane's head when I should visit her that afternoon. Now I was in a dilemma, for I do not make promises lightly. When I asked Lucy about this, she suggested that as the mother believed in divine healing perhaps I should lay my hands on her head, by proxy as it were. This I decided to do.

I arrived punctually. Jane's mother opened the door and we chatted a few moments in the hall. She said she would take me up and introduce me to her daughter, but would not stay with us though she would only be in the adjoining room. Later I was to hear she spent the whole hour while I was with Jane, in prayer; this was a perfect setting. Before we went upstairs she did not mention anything about not laying hands on Jane's head, but tapping her finger lightly on the palm of her other hand, she begged me not so much as to touch Jane's bed like that, as jarring could cause her so much pain. Naturally, I agreed to this.

Talking with Jane, I soon discovered they were a committed Christian family, and we got on well from the start. Soon I was telling her of miracles Jesus had done in my own ministry in South Africa, and in so doing was able to get across, I hoped, the scriptural basis for the Church's healing work. It is ever necessary to engender faith in those who need help, not faith in oneself as a healer, but in Jesus who is the only Healer, and the fact that sometimes He uses us. After all, since He had used me in the past, why not now?

At the end of an hour, during which I felt at least she had her mind taken from herself, I felt the time had come to pray. Her only movements had been fairly frequent head movements as she lay flat on her divan bed, no pillow, so she could turn left or right easily; with each turn, as she swallowed she winced with pain. I told her about my promise not to actually lay hands on her head, but that I felt led to do this with her permission. She smilingly agreed, as I assured her it would be very gently done. I did not know until some days later that while I had been witnessing to Jesus and speaking the Word, Jane had already begun to feel something happening at the back of her neck. Thus she felt I would not hurt her, for already the Lord was in control.

There was just room for me to get behind her divan which had no headboard, and I could then bend over without touching the divan itself. I prayed aloud for about three minutes, my hands resting gently upon her head as she lay with her eyes closed in prayer herself. There was insufficient room to kneel, and as the divan was low it was somewhat back-breaking, and maybe speaking very slowly would enable time to pass less painfully for me.

After my prayer ended I remained with my hands on her head for about two more minutes. Jane opened her eyes, and I said, 'How did it feel?' She grinned and said one word: 'Heavenly!' In fact, it was more heavenly than either of us knew at that moment. It is because of the subsequent questions of the medical men that I give details of what I did, as they just couldn't understand. In fact, I never have done anything more than that, unless it be anointing with oil. To try to manipulate any part of the physical make up would be criminal and dangerous, for I have no knowledge or authority for such practices. This, too, I mention because what happened after I left the house was certainly not my work, though surely an answer to our prayers and, if I may say so, to the actual laying on of hands in this particular case.

Jane would not let me leave as she said her mother would have a cup of tea ready quickly, and I could chat briefly over it. I recall her mother thanking me and then saying an odd thing: 'I tried to contact several people before I rang the Mission, but as soon as I heard your voice I knew you were the right person to come . . . and you did!'

Jane herself had no tea, but her hitherto pale face had become very rosy after prayer. This to me was a small but sure sign she had received a blessing, whether physical or spiritual I didn't know, and I sometimes call it 'radiant heat'; I believe it to be a touch from the Lord in whose name alone we pray. Others speak of vibrations, the same wave-length, or other things which really don't interest me. We often make too much of both our feelings and outward signs, and not enough of the gracious Lord who works in varied ways. The details given in this account are given because to me they were relevant to a kind of healing I had never known before. In point of fact, for many weeks afterwards, whenever I placed my hands on Jane's head, even at a mission service when our thoughts may or may not have been centred on any need of her own, but on the need of someone else, her head would invariably begin to move gently to one side; this was not due to any manipulating by me, and often I could feel her trying not to let it happen . . . in vain!

Suddenly her mother and I were startled. Jane jerked herself up in bed, grabbed the collar round her neck and flung it to the bottom of her bed, then flopped back flushed with the exertion. It was so sudden and unexpected we were frightened. 'Are you all right?' asked her mother anxiously. 'Was it a pain?' I echoed, thinking if it was her mother might soon find I'd broken my promise and would blame me! Jane said, 'No. But I'm so terribly hot I can't stand that thing any more.'

As onlookers we were relieved when soon after Jane said: 'There's something queer taking place at the back of my neck, and it doesn't hurt at all.' And as we kept our gaze on her she spoke again, 'It's fantastic! . . . it's as if someone is gently doing something to my vertebrae, my muscles, my strings . . . and it's marvellous.' Her radiant face dispelled all our fears. I rose, put my cup and saucer down, saying, 'The Holy Spirit is already at work. You don't need me any more.'

Her mother came down to let me out, and as I walked to the Underground station in the sunshine several people gave me an odd look as they passed. Whether it was the light of joy on my face, or they overheard the Holy Spirit bubbling forth in an unknown tongue praise to Christ, for whom He has such a passion of love, I shall never know. What I did know I shared with Bill Wood, the Missioner, on my return, at which he called the staff members together and we had a praise meeting on our own. I felt sure I would hear good news next morning, but it didn't come. I couldn't believe some healing had not taken place.

After lunch I was called to the phone to hear, I thought, Jane's mother, but found it was Jane speaking. It went like this:

'How are you, Jane?'

'Fine, thanks.'

A pause. No information volunteered. So I spoke again: 'Had a good night?'

She replied: 'Yes thanks, very good indeed.'

Still no information. Then, warily, I said, 'I don't recall you had a telephone beside your bed?'

It was then she laughed, saying, 'I'm not in bed. I'm up and dressed. In fact I'm standing by the telephone.'

Now for weeks she had been mostly confined to bed, and since the towel episode had not been allowed to even put a foot to the floor under doctor's orders.

'Jane!' I said, 'it's too soon . . . you shouldn't be up yet.'

'Oh, that's all right,' she answered, 'I've cooked the dinner today! Actually, I had thought to clean the car, but decided that was a bit too much for a start.'

Her mother then took the receiver from her, and from then on they alternated in telling me what had happened since I left them. By the time she returned to Jane after seeing me out, she found her happily moving her head in easy movements as if doing gentle exercises. 'Don't do that,' she said anxiously, 'you'll hurt yourself.' 'But I'm not doing it, Mother,' she replied, 'it's just as if someone is doing it for me, and it doesn't hurt a bit!' It was true she was still lying on her divan, but even so the movements did not tire her, and went on more or less for an hour, by which time they suddenly realised Jane had somehow moved up the divan so that her head was over the end of it, making circular movements the more easily.

Soon after this Jane felt she should get up, and it would be natural after so long on her back with so much pain for her to be somewhat unsteady. Yet it was not so, and once she was standing up, her arms began to move round like a windmill. Again her mother was alarmed, thinking she was showing off, and cried, 'Don't do that. You might hurt yourself.' Back came the reply: 'But Mother, I'm not doing it of my own volition, and it doesn't hurt.' As her mother said to me, 'A few nights ago I had watched for four hours the agony of Jane's head turning back to front, and now, for about three hours, I watched a divine healing taking place under my very nose!'

Jane's friend and flat-mate, Millie, had seen something of the healing in process when she came home from work. At seven o'clock Jane went back to bed, having spent the hours alternating the exercises; when she was tired of standing and waving her arms, she would sit on a chair and her head would gently loll back and forth and round about, and she felt no pain. After a refreshing sleep for two hours she awoke, and Millie excitedly got on Jane's divan as she lay on it, and as she jumped up and down in no light manner she was crying out: 'You're healed! You're healed!' And this was the bed I had promised not to touch however lightly because Jane could not stand the pain!

In the days that followed I admit to concern over the kind of healing that had taken place; it seemed akin to the things spiritualists claim for their mediums, that is, unseen spirit guides are at work. It was a while before a dear friend of mine, strongly opposed to spiritualism and much used in healing by our Lord, told me how after an accident he experienced literally hundreds and hundreds of times what he described as a sharp little pull at his extremities. The accident had left him with what he termed 'a curvature of the spine the wrong way round'. For months and months after an initial divine healing which occurred when a vicar prayed for him in the name of Jesus, my friend said whenever he lay and stretched himself, arms behind his head, he would feel this tiny tug in finger-tips and feet. At the end of this period his curvature had straightened out, and he was as upright as any man. This dispelled my concern. I also mention this because Jane for a long time after the initial healing had cramping in her neck, which she said was quite involuntary. God used natural laws to complete the healing He began so dramatically; after all, He not only invented the laws but makes them work. Now, after eight years, those neck muscles were receiving life-blood, and this happened during those painful cramping occasions, but Jane didn't mind that, knowing her muscles were growing again to do their own work. Within a week of her initial healing her neck circumference grew more than an inch. Today her neck has one hundred per cent movement—such a blessing, not least when she drives her car

—and her healing cannot be denied. No man did this, and whatever was needed was done by the Holy Spirit to manifest Jesus as Healer. What skilled and clever men had not been able to do in three weeks, or looking back eight years, in fifteen months, was accomplished by God in five minutes, initially, and then gradually. Over and above the physical healing one cannot measure what it meant to Jane herself. Her faith in the healing Christ became ever stronger, her witness to Him ever better, and many have known blessing because her prayer life has been enriched.

Now Jane and I have much the same sort of sense of humour. The second day following her healing she was given the thought to make a generous gift to the Mission which I represent. The Lord told her, she said, quite clearly, how much to give. It was a considerable sum. She was elated at the thought, for the Mission never takes collections, receives nothing from Church or State financially, but relies on the Lord to provide; it is in fact a charity.

Thinking it over, she thought perhaps she could give it a year hence, for she had been saving up a long time in order to have a holiday in Rome. She was just thinking she could postpone the gift when she had a really sharp twinge of pain in the back of her neck, the first since her healing. 'All right, Lord,' she said, 'I'll give it now!' She never had a pain like that again. She wasn't able to go to Rome either. And when she told me about it we laughed together. How good it is that He has a sense of humour. Many a time in my ministry has mine saved a situation, but I never heard of Him jab anyone like that before. But then, in the healing and deliverance ministry one is often learning something new, and also more of Him who knows we toil for those who suffer much in body, mind and spirit, and that is why He sometimes gives us laughs, or we could never take the strain.

Public healing services are only held at the London

Healing Mission on Thursdays, so that we are never guilty of drawing people away from their own churches on Sundays. People come to us from many denominations since sickness is not peculiar to any particular one, and they often come because they get no help from their own church where healing is not practised. We teach them about Christ as both Saviour and Healer, and hope they may learn something to take with them to those of their own churches.

Nowadays there are more healing services taking place in Christian churches than at any other time in history, but there are yet far too many priests and pastors who feel that the supernatural healing work of the Holy Spirit in the Church must be relegated to the time when Jesus walked the earth and healed the sick Himself, or to the first thirty-five years of Church history briefly covered by the Acts of the Apostles. Since there is ample evidence that healings took place during the first four centuries of the Christian era, written evidence from men of no mean spiritual stature, this is a strange anomaly. While it remains there will always be a need for the London Healing Mission. The very fact that a seemingly never-ending queue wends its way quietly to it, speaks for itself.

I recall an earnest Christian worker who once came to the Mission for an evening service and remained to talk afterward, as our custom is, over a cup of tea. The fellowship is real, and there are always those who will gladly give their quiet testimony of the Healing Christ because they have themselves been healed. This woman came to find out for herself, and was somewhat suspicious; a mutual lady friend brought her, and like Philip to Nathaniel of old had said: 'Come and see'. Her suspicion evaporated, and on the way home she enthused over all she had heard and seen. She kept saying, 'But I can't get over it. After service everyone was talking about the Lord; no matter who they were or where they'd come from, they all talked about the Lord. Now, in our church, some go, some stay and chat after service, but no one ever talks about the Lord!' Maybe that is why so many love the Mission, because there He made His love known to them in a special way, for it is His Mission, and there we honour His name, not only for what He does within its walls, but because of who He is.

Several years after Jane's healing, at the end of an evening service, she fell heavily down the last few steps that lead from the ground floor to the chapel and its adjoining rooms below. At the time a number of people were chatting or collecting their tea, others having gone straight home. I heard the crash but did not at once go to see what had happened, as others were there to help; nor had I any idea who had fallen. A few minutes later I was called, and found Jane more or less knocked out, her toes caught awkwardly on the last stair; as it happened capable people were to hand.

In addition to Bill Wood, the Missioner, were members of staff and, from the congregation, a nursing sister, another lady who had previously done years of hospital work, a man who knew about St John Ambulance work, and several others. I was shocked to find it was Jane because I knew it could have done untold harm to her neck. She was lying on the stone floor amid broken crockery, a nasty bruise on her temple where she had struck her head on the corner of the table which held the cups, and her face deathly pale. I knelt beside her and asked: 'Jane, is it your neck?'

'No,' she whispered, 'it's my knee . . . I've dislocated my knee.'

Indeed, we could see the patella some four inches below the knee under the skin, looking rather like a mouse in shape. Shock, torn ligaments, intense pain, all because she half turned on the stair holding her tea-cup in one hand, and then felt as if someone had caught her legs from under her. We were all distressed, and in some uncertainty of what to do for the best. The sister took charge.

She released Jane's feet and tied her legs together, then we raised her on to the long cushion from a studio couch which was better than the stone floor. It was surprising she had not been cut by broken china, especially the halves of a cup with jagged points which were under her.

There was now some discussion among the half-dozen helpers as to whether one should ring for a doctor or an ambulance, since obviously it was a surgical matter. I did say a brief, silent prayer that pain would be taken away, but then became involved with the others and heard much about the merits and demerits of various hospitals mentioned by different people!

Finally, I climbed the stairs to the office where a lady was already thumbing the telephone directory for 'Hospitals'. As we were deciding which one to ring, a friend poked his head round the door and said, 'Jane wants you to come down and pray for her before you ring the hospital.'

'All right,' I said, 'though actually I did say a short silent prayer earlier. Still, it is a matter for a surgeon, but maybe while I delay the Lord will show us which hospital to send her to.'

Descending the stairs, I found the others grouped round Jane, and was told there were more people praying for her in the chapel as they had not yet left. Kneeling, I placed one hand on Jane's knee, the other on the displaced patella. I felt conscious of a spiritual atmosphere, for all present were believing and praying Christians. Then I said aloud a very short prayer for healing. Opening my eyes, I suddenly felt intensely irritated—I didn't know why. I felt annoyed with myself and the others all gathered round. To myself I thought: 'This is ridiculous. Here we are, all believers in divine healing, and we know jolly well Jesus heals, and we should be expecting a miracle; in fact, we should expect a miracle every day.'

Without a word from anyone I climbed the stairs to

call for an ambulance, but as I reached the top of the short flight I heard a little scream and a stirring of people. Once more the same head appeared round the corner and the owner cried, 'Come back, come back!' I promptly did so, but was too late to see what the others had all seen. Opening their eyes after prayer, they saw Jane's patella begin to move very slowly up the leg, then it turned left and when it came to the bone it just hopped over and into its correct position. You can imagine the excitement and the joy. The lady who had done years of nursing apologised, for it was she who had screamed, as she couldn't contain herself.

As for Jane, she rested a week and was back at work. Of course, it could have been an operation and much pain, and some six weeks away from her own essential hospital work, but the Lord spared her all that.

It was sometime later that one of our Prayer Group members, talking about Jane's mishaps, said: 'She's very unlucky in some ways, isn't she? And yet in another way she's jolly lucky.' To which I replied, 'I know what you mean, but luck is a word I never use myself, for it has no place in Divine Healing.'

We can all learn from the various happenings when healings take place, and in this particular healing, what must have been obvious to everyone was the clear illustration of the value of a group of believers concentrating on a particular need. Perhaps the irritation I felt was an awareness of my own lack of faith. Happily for Jane, others had it if I didn't! So we praised God from whom all blessings flow.

## 11  FRANCIS

The morning mail brought a piteous cry from a mother's heart which could not fail to move my own. It was not for herself, but for an only son called Francis. She said she and her husband were full-time workers in the Salvation Army. Three years ago, when Francis was nearly thirteen, he was playing cricket and was struck a blow with the hard ball which robbed him of sight in one eye. Now, just three weeks ago, he had been playing cricket when a ball struck him in the good eye, blinding him as before. Medical opinion was quite definite; the boy would never see again. The second accident was a replica of the first. He was totally blind.

Putting the letter on my desk, my mind went back to my own boyhood. I loved cricket as a fair all-rounder in the game, and when away at school captained the House team; I also captained a church team in my youth, and as a curate formed a team in the parish. Only when faulty vision necessitated my wearing spectacles did I finally give up cricket with regret. My sympathies were with Francis; moreover my first name is also Francis. I felt we had something in common. He lived some 235 miles from London, but if his parents brought him to us we could minister to him. On the other hand, distance is no barrier to healing if the prayer of faith is strong enough to close the gap.

From the letter I could picture all she described. No

longer able to go to school, unable to see a single thing, Francis sat at home in misery. She said they had been sitting in their lounge together a few evenings ago, feeling crushed and oppressed. The future seemed as dark as the present. No one spoke. Then, unexpectedly, the fifteen-year-old said, 'Mum, do you believe that Jesus Christ can heal today?'

Surprised, she replied somewhat hesitatingly, 'Well, y-e-s, yes I do believe that.' Whereupon Francis, going to the core of the matter, said, 'Ah . . . but do you believe that He *does* heal today?'

Gaining some confidence herself she was able to reply, 'Yes, son, I do. Sometimes we read in newspapers of a miracle taking place. There are people who practise healing, but in the Army we don't.'

No more was said, but she decided to make enquiries without telling Francis. Three days later she happened to meet her brother, and asked him if he knew of anyone practising healing. He told her there was a place in London somewhere, couldn't remember the name of it, but had a feeling he might even have a leaflet about it. 'Mind you,' he said, 'it's a long time ago, before the war, and maybe they don't do it any more, or maybe they have moved elsewhere.'

He searched through his papers and came across a London Healing Mission leaflet many years old, even discoloured with age. She wrote, and so by letter we had contact. A day or so later I was able to speak to a schoolboy who regularly worshipped at our Mission. He was just a year younger than the blind boy and his name, too, was Francis. I told him of the tragic letter and suggested he might care to pray privately for the boy he had never met, and asked him to receive the laying on of hands for him by proxy every Thursday at our normal service. He agreed, and I wrote to tell of our decision, and as the blind Francis would also pray we would be a 'Franciscan trio'. It was the following Thursday we began in this way.

A week later I had another letter from the mother. She told how they had been sitting in their lounge when at our Mission I ministered for her blind son. 'Suddenly,' she wrote, 'Francis cried out: "I can see something!" '

'What can you see, son?' they asked.

'A tiny speck of light,' he said, pointing toward the fireplace.

'You're pointing at the fire, is it that you can see?'

'Oh, no! I can only see a tiny speck of light, but it's the first bit of light I've seen since my accident four weeks ago.'

In London we were quite unaware of this, and also of the fact that the parents were bringing their son to a famous London eye hospital two days later. The mother in her second letter told of their renewed hope that something might be done to restore sight to the eye damaged a few weeks before; the specialist in their home town could offer no hope himself, but suggested they came to London to make quite sure about his verdict. He was humble enough to do so, and perhaps they would hear of some possible chance for renewed vision. Thus they came.

They told the doctor of the speck of light Francis now had. He listened, and then took the boy for examination. Then returning with him he spoke regretfully: 'I'm sorry, but it would be wrong of me to give you false hopes. He will never see again. True, there is a tiny speck of light but it is very small, and cannot possibly grow any larger. Moreover, it is only temporary, and soon he will be in complete darkness again.' They were shattered after their hopes, but the doctor spoke kindly to Francis and urged him to learn Braille, of course, and to plan for his future. In her letter to me his mother ended with the words, 'Please, please continue to pray for our son. We do believe in Jesus.'

I told our Francis in London what had happened, and again he promised he would continue to pray faithfully in his private prayers, as well as come regularly to the Mission as proxy for blind Francis. There was no further word from the saddened home.

Three months passed. Once more it was our Thursday evening service at the Mission; kneeling before me at the end of the row was a tall boy who looked up and said, 'For my eyes, please. I've had accidents.' He looked all right to me. I saw no white stick, and no one had led him down the narrow aisle to the sanctuary, so I gathered he had some vision anyway. I prayed accordingly for full healing.

After the service I stood in the garden outside the chapel as the worshippers left, and seeing a happy couple who were strangers, asked them to wait so we could have a word together. They said they intended to, as it was their son Francis I had just prayed for. Even then it didn't dawn on me that they were our hitherto unseen friends from the north. My wife then took them across to our nearby flat, and there I joined them. Entering the room I crossed to this tall lad, putting my hand out in greeting. He shook it at once . . . then he could really see!

'Francis,' I cried, 'can you really see my ugly face?'

He grinned, 'Sure! I can.'

We all laughed with such joy. They had refrained from telling us of the very slow but sure improvement of the vision in his eye, but now they had come once more to the hospital in London. After examination the doctor was so excited he said, 'Do you realise that this boy's eye has more than half its full vision back? It's a miracle! A miracle!' and he called in other staff members to hear the good news.

We continued to pray for full restoration of sight. Our Francis in London was as thrilled as anyone. Indeed, he had learnt at the age of fifteen what I had not known till I was fifty; that one can be a channel by faith and prayer for the physical healing of someone you have never seen, and who lives hundreds of miles from you.

Such an idea had simply escaped me until I was brought into this healing ministry.

Two months later they came again; for they had now moved to the south and so were nearer to us. Once more in our flat we had happy fellowship; and we learnt his sight was still improving. When the time came for them to leave I walked into the lounge to find his mother standing alone, eyes closed, moving her head slowly from side to side.

'What are you moving your head like that for?' I asked.

Opening her eyes, she smiled: 'Oh, I was just thinking,' she said, 'five months ago our son, the only child we ever had, was totally blind—he couldn't see a thing! And now he can see, and moreover he even has a job!' —she paused, then added with another smile, 'and what is more, he is earning more than his mum and dad put together!'

A few years have passed since then. Today, Francis can see with both his eyes, and he has passed his car driving test at the first attempt.

Long ago in Nazareth, Jesus said: 'The Spirit of the Lord is upon me . . . he hath sent me to heal the broken-hearted, to preach . . . recovering of sight to the blind . . .' (Luke 4 : 18).

Truly we can say as He did: 'This day is this scripture fulfilled . . .'

## 12 STEPHEN AND NIGEL

Friday at the London Healing Mission often seems to be a day when the staff are in a mood for fun and laughter. This is not to say we do not laugh at other times, nor do I think it is a reaction to the healing services we hold on Thursdays. We have sometimes talked about it ourselves, this sense of uplift, if not to say gaiety, but it remains a mystery as to why we become so light-hearted. On that day there are usually more of us present for one thing; one has also to admit that having been kept busy on mission work all the week we could be affected by the prospect of a weekend break. Such a break is needful because we are constantly being reminded of the sorrows and sicknesses of people who visit us, write to us, or telephone. The very nature of our work involves us with people in need, and since our task is to counsel and pray for them we must be ready to listen to their stories, some of which can be depressing and, at times, heart-breaking. Without compassion we can help no one.

So maybe we brighten somewhat visibly on a Friday at the thought of a change; and it can have nothing to do with a weekend wage packet since most of the staff give their services freely for the love they have toward Jesus. Whatever the cause, frequently on Fridays someone or something starts us off in joyous laughter which of itself brings release, and with it a subtle drawing together in the unity of the Spirit which is the bond of peace. This ability to laugh as well as cry, to praise as well as pray, is something to thank God for, and there is ample opportunity to do both when engaged in the ministry of healing.

It was on such a Friday in the month of January that the week's work was ending; it had been a happy day, and staff members were on the point of leaving. They usually go about 4 p.m., and it was just before the hour when Kathleen, one of our secretaries, came into the hall and found me there.

'There's a telephone message for you,' she said, 'it's your son-in-law, Bill.'

'That's strange,' I exclaimed. 'They don't have a phone. Anyway, put it through to the study and I'll talk to him from there.' As I turned to go she stopped me with the words: 'No, he's not on the phone now. He hadn't time to wait, but said he'd ring later. He rang to ask for prayer. I'm afraid it's not good news.'

'What's happened?' I asked.

'It's Stephen, your little grandson,' she replied.

'Stephen,' I echoed, 'what's the trouble?'

'He's very poorly,' she said, 'and they've rushed him to hospital. They rang your son-in-law at work, and he was actually on his way to the hospital when he rang.'

A picture of Stephen flashed across my mind; an endearing little boy with fair hair, only two years and two months old, a gentle-natured child, and our only grandson.

'What's wrong with him?' I asked.

'It's serious,' she answered gently as if to soften the blow, 'he has mumps and meningitis.'

I could scarcely believe it; but it was true. I thanked Kathleen for giving me the message, and asked her and the other members of staff to remember him in their prayers over the weekend. They readily agreed. Lucy was out, and our younger daughter was at work. As the front door closed on the departing staff the house became suddenly silent. I went into my study and shut the door. Mumps, I thought. Well, a childish ailment, and a painful one. I remembered Lucy had it at Christmas some years after we were married, and it's always worse when one gets a childish ailment as an adult. Even so, there could be no real problem about mumps.

But meningitis—that was a different matter altogether. When combined with mumps or measles it can be terribly dangerous, even fatal. I told myself Stephen was in hospital; doctors and nurses would give of their best. But, would it be good enough? Thoughtfully I stood gazing through the study window at the quiet garden scene beyond. It struck me how quickly a few words can change everything. The happy laughter, the talk of the day, and the singing that had come from the kitchen while someone prepared lunch were as if they had never been. The wintry rays of the January sun were still shedding their light, but it was pale and held no warmth. The leafless branches of neighbouring trees, which even in winter often seem friendly disposed towards me, now appeared cold and lifeless. Though it was warm in my study I felt chilled. Far away, Stephen, so young and tender, was battling against a powerful evil thing that sought to destroy him. What chance had he, I asked myself, against the enemy of mankind? In the natural, I was forced to admit, very little. True, he might survive, but in what sort of mental and physical condition? Meningitis with mumps may leave the victim alive, but in such condition of mind and body that death might be more merciful. So my thoughts ran on at speed in a negative vein, for I was emotionally involved and the enemy was attacking me too. Doubt and apprehension endeavour to make their unwelcome intrusion so to disarm us in our fight against the foe. Jesus knew this testing in His own experience; why should not we, who follow Him? As for those who don't know Him,

I often wonder how they cope with life's shocks and sorrows.

Well, by grace I had come to know something of His power to heal, not only through those of the medical profession, but by the supernatural power of His Holy Spirit. He had at times used me to bring healing to the sick, even providing the necessary compassion for sick people who were strangers to me. He had even healed people from a distance, and what He had done before He could do again.

Stephen was a hundred and forty miles away, but distance is nothing to God who is omnipresent. In the crises of the very young, time too can be of tremendous importance where life and death are concerned; but time is nothing to God who is eternal. As to that, I was wasting my time in soliloquy. I needed to talk to the devil, and to God, not to myself.

Now anger rose up within me; not toward God, as may happen, but toward the prince of this world who comes to destroy and to kill. I slid to my knees and looked out and up to that stratum around the earth where the spiritual battles are fought, of which the greatest of all Christian missionaries wrote to his converts in Ephesus : 'We wrestle not against flesh and blood, but against principalities, against powers, against the rulers of the darkness of this world, against wicked spirits in the heavenlies' (Eph. 6 : 12).

There is such a thing as righteous anger, and in that vein I addressed the enemy aloud in strong terms, telling him that I came against him from my position in Christ, and with the authority of Christ. I reminded him that he is a defeated foe, and that we have been given authority and power by Jesus to 'tread upon serpents and scorpions and over all the power of the enemy'. Then I told him in no uncertain terms in the all-powerful name of Jesus to take his hands off our grandson, and to clear off and take the sickness with him, and forbade him to return.

I then spoke to our Heavenly Father in simple faith after this fashion: 'Father, you know all about Stephen. He is dear to Lucy and me, dearer still to Bill and Mary, our daughter, but dearest of all to you, for you made him for yourself. I don't believe you gave him to them in order to snatch him away after only two years. Yet because he is yours first, you can do what you will with him. You can even take him right now—and I'd rather you did that than leave him to be like a mental cabbage, unable to think or talk coherently, and so remain a burden to himself and to all who would have the care of him in the years ahead. So, Father, I am quite deliberately putting Stephen into your loving hands now, and I *mean* that, so you may do with him what you will, for your will is best. But I think it is your will to heal him, so I ask you to, in Jesus' name. Thank you, Father. Amen.'

I had only spent about five minutes on my knees, and as I rose to my feet I felt a warm glow in my chest. What we feel is not so important, but I was comforted by this physical sensation which was something new to me.

Later, Bill rang and told us their doctor had diagnosed mumps at his surgery the previous day. Stephen's condition worsened that evening and he had a bad night. Bill went to work early next morning leaving Mary to see to the children. She became so concerned about Stephen that at 10.30 a.m. she rang from a kiosk down the road and asked for the doctor to call, which he promised to do on his rounds.

As the hours progressed the child persisted in lying flat, refusing even to raise his head from the pillow because of the pain; and soon rigidity was caused by the meningitis going up the back of the neck to the brain. It was after 3.30 p.m. that the doctor arrived, hardly expecting anything more than a painful condition from mumps. He immediately went down the road and telephoned for an ambulance, and wrote his diagnosis for the isolation hospital doctor. Stephen screamed with the pain when the ambulance men lifted him up. Mary rang Bill to tell him everything, and he promptly left work and drove to the hospital, arriving just at four o'clock as the ambulance brought his son through the gates. On the way he had stopped to ring the Mission to ask us to pray, but found he only had a single coin in his pocket, a sixpence. This sufficed to give him ten seconds on STD, but it proved a life-saver! It was just after four o'clock that I rebuked the enemy and prayed for Stephen in my study.

We told Bill not to ring again till Saturday night as we had a bi-monthly Saturday afternoon meeting at the Mission. During that meeting we had a short time for ministry. I suggested Lucy should receive healing for Stephen by proxy, and two people stood beside her and prayed for him. Then the fifty-five people present kept silent for two minutes as we prayerfully lifted up the child to God for healing, picturing him as God made him to be, well and happy.

That evening after everyone had gone home, Lucy told me she had prayed a strange prayer while we were all praying silently in the chapel. It went like this: 'Father, thank you for the healing of Stephen, which I now claim in the name of Jesus. And, Father, so that you may have all the glory, will you please let it be known that the healing took place within the hour.'

Later, Bill rang to say the isolation hospital doctor had confirmed the original diagnosis, and had added that he was mystified: Stephen, he said, had every symptom known to medical science of mumps with meningitis. We concluded that as a child's condition can change rapidly for better or worse, the doctor was unwilling at this stage to give any opinion as to the final outcome. Meantime we told Bill not to ring again until this was forthcoming. In London we continued to pray.

Tuesday evening Mary rang and I answered the phone. She was terribly excited and the tone of her voice was sufficient to know it was good news. 'You'll never guess what's happened about Stephen,' she cried.

'Well, what is it?' I asked. 'It sounds good.'

'Well,' she reiterated, 'you'll never guess what it is!'

'Tell me then!' I urged. 'We're palpitating here to know the news.'

'Stephen is home!' she cried exultantly.

'Home? What for?' I queried, for I was puzzled.

'He's had a healing . . . he's healed! . . . he hasn't even got any swelling from mumps!' she cried.

'What, already?' I said in astonishment. True, I was supposed to be believing for Stephen's healing! Indeed, I was . . . but not that much! I put the phone through to Lucy so that she could hear the glad news. How we praised God!

Mary told her how their vicar had kindly agreed to act as a go-between in case of any emergency, for he had a phone and could bring her any hospital message. They had also prayed for Stephen in their church on Sunday. When the vicar had a hospital call quite early on Tuesday and was asked if he would take a message about Stephen his heart sank:

'What is it?' he asked.

Came the reply: 'Would you please ask his mother to come and fetch him home.'

Puzzled, he said 'Home? . . . What for?'

'Well,' said the nurse, 'he seems to be all right now, and the doctor thinks he might as well be home as he's fretting for his mother.'

The vicar said he nearly dropped the phone in astonishment. Indeed the news seemed too good to be true.

One interesting thing was the varied reactions of people to the news of the healing. Some from the church when they heard the news said: 'Well, it couldn't have been meningitis then!', whereas others who never go to church, when they heard of the healing said: 'Now isn't that wonderful! God is good!' Maybe there's a lesson in this somewhere.

Mary chatted at length over the phone, and told how she had collected Stephen and spoken with the hospital doctor once more. Again he said, 'We both know—your doctor and I—that this little boy had every symptom known to medical science of mumps with meningitis. Yet I was mystified, for he was brought in at four o'clock, but there was a delay of an hour; I didn't see him until five o'clock, but when I did, I knew that *something had happened within the hour*, for the rigidity to the brain had already gone.' Neither Mary nor the doctor knew his words were the exact fulfilment of Lucy's Saturday prayer. Because there is no time with God, the lesson here is that God can use today's prayer yesterday, which is an encouragement for us who intercede.

So Stephen came home. True, he was supposed to be kept in bed a while, but not likely! He trotted around after his mother whenever she left his room, determined not to lose sight of her, and who can blame him after the loneliness of an isolation room all to himself. He has never looked back since that day, and whereas he was somewhat slow to talk previously, he has more than made up for it since. I recollect Bill saying over the phone during the crisis period, 'If you had seen Stephen yesterday [the day he went to hospital] you wouldn't have given him the slightest possible chance of recovery.' Praise God for the miracle!

The healing of Stephen took place in January, and it was fourteen months later that I preached at a church in the Manchester diocese one Sunday night. After service there was a 'follow-up' in the nearby hall for fellowship. After the usual drinking of tea on such occasions, there was a period for questions—I often answer them by telling more stories of healing to the glory of God.

On this occasion a woman halfway down the hall called out and asked for prayer for a little boy, the son of one of the Young Wives from their Fellowship. She said he had meningitis. I asked how old he was, and she said 'Two and a half years.' Quite naturally, I then told them the story of Stephen's healing. I gathered little Nigel had been taken ill the previous Wednesday, and was rushed to hospital the following day. Now it was Sunday night; this was a much longer period of delay than in the case of Stephen.

When I had ended my story of Stephen—which, of course, the Lord could use to engender faith in the seventy or more people present in the hall—I asked if they were all agreeable that we should now pray for Nigel. An affirmative silence seemed to be the answer, so I asked them to just bow their heads and close their eyes, and lifting up my arms we became absolutely silent for the space of about one minute. Then, as in Stephen's case, I firmly rebuked the enemy and commanded him to take his evil work from this little boy who belonged to Jesus; after this I prayed aloud for his complete healing in the name of Jesus. I suppose I prayed for two minutes, and then asked everyone present to hold up this child silently for God to touch him, visualising him healthy and happy as God meant him to be. I ended this group ministry by saying aloud: 'Thank you, Father, in Jesus' name. Amen.'

Next day I left the parish and spent two days with relatives in Cheshire. From their home on Wednesday I rang up the vicarage where I had been for the weekend. The vicar's wife told me she had been to the hospital on Monday afternoon and had found the mother at Nigel's bedside. Somehow she had felt sure the vicar's wife would come that afternoon, and she was able to tell her that on Sunday night Nigel had fallen asleep at precisely 9 p.m. It was the first deep sleep he had had since he became so ill the previous Wednesday. The vicar's wife then told her what I had said, and how we had all prayed for her child, and she was understandably grateful. When he awoke on Monday morning he was better. On Tuesday she took him home fully restored after his viral meningitis.

It was on the Monday night at a meeting of church leaders that one of the church councillors, who rejoiced with the others to learn of answered prayer for the sick child, said he could confirm the healing. He had deliberately looked at his watch in the hall on Sunday night as I began to pray, and it was exactly five minutes to nine. One minute of silence, two minutes for prayer, then two more minutes in which we all shared in holding up this little boy in faith to God. And as I thanked God, the little fellow in hospital some miles away fell into a deep healing sleep. In the morning he was well.

The Word of God tells us to resist the devil (1 Pet. 5:8, 9); adding that we are in a position to do so strongly when we are 'steadfast in the faith'. Indeed both Peter and James tell us to put the enemy to flight (Jas. 4:7): for this, our submission to the Lord is necessary, along with clean living. To do this work one must know how to protect oneself with the Blood of Jesus Christ, or one could be routed by the enemy (cf. Acts 19:13–17).

As to the handing over of a loved one 'in sickness or in health' to our heavenly Father by a deliberate act of faith, this is never easy; but as we advance spiritually we can come to a place where, by grace, we really believe that God's love for our dear ones is greater than our own. Thus He may restore a loved one to us, or take him to Himself. We may even truly say: 'The Lord gave ... the Lord hath taken away ... blessed be the name of the Lord.'

Come to think of it, God the Father, because He 'so loved the world' (John 3:16) entrusted His only begotten Son Jesus Christ to mankind: and we know what they did to Him. When Jesus Himself came to a full realisation of both the challenge and the sacrifice of His own life for ours, He did not fail His Father or us. He said He had come to give his life a ransom for many, and so He did. There is, then, no limit to the infinite Love of God for those who accept in faith Jesus His Son as their

Saviour. Therefore we who profess such faith should not find it too great a challenge to put ourselves and our loved ones, whether in health or in sickness, into the hands of Almighty God. Indeed there is nowhere better to be, now and for ever.

## 13 NADINE

It was one of those hot August days when it is good to be able to leave the crowded thoroughfares of London, albeit by coach, and get away from buildings and traffic into more peaceful surroundings. I found myself appreciating the rare chance of being able to laze comfortably in a deck chair in a vicarage garden, while my hostess, the young vicar's wife, chatted easily about Jesus, and the subject of divine healing. It was evident that she had a simple faith, and a very busy life, for there were three young children to cater and care for, and a lovely baby who slept in a pram nearby. Add to that a husband, and a parish, and you have all the ingredients to make the kind of life it is impossible to imagine, only experience. The constant calls upon one's time, and presence, at all sorts of church functions and services, and the frequent callers both at the door and on the telephone, made life busier than God meant it to be. Yet, I felt as I listened to her that she had a right attitude to the life that was so full of other people, and in spite of the many problems, her own as well as those brought to the vicarage by others, she would take them not only philosophically, but also with that grace which God provides for such as serve Him where He guides.

We had never met before, nor as yet had I seen her husband who, she informed me, would be glad to see me later though he was unwell, and in bed. The purpose of my visit was to see and hear about Nadine, and then to minister to her. The two older children disappeared from the scene, the baby slept, and that left Nadine to her own devices. She was sixteen months old, tiny for her age I felt, with fair hair and good colour in her cheeks; she was also very lively with a mind of her own, and if she was pushed around at times by the older ones it was all part of a toughening process which, I thought, she stood up to very well. Yet Nadine had a great disadvantage, for when she was born she had only one hip socket, with the result that one leg was rather like an appendage of comparatively little use.

Her mother explained that in such cases nature might well provide in due time the missing socket; meanwhile the other socket and leg grow in the normal way. It takes a long time for a socket to form, so it means one leg will be an inch or more shorter than the other, assuming it does eventually thicken at the femur and so become fixed in the hip socket correctly. Naturally, they longed for the socket to grow quickly, for the leg to become fixed therein, and for this child to be like any normal child, able to walk without a limp.

'You must have seen people from time to time,' she said, 'who walk badly and bend their body sideways from the hip; this is often because they were born without a hip socket on one side.' I confessed to my ignorance about such matters, but realised this little girl might be very crippled if indeed the socket failed to grow, or even failed to grow quickly enough so that the leg might find its rightful place in time to save her from lameness. To picture this little child being unable to walk, or even if walking, being so lame that she could not run and take part in games like other children in the years ahead, tended to cast a shadow over the pleasant scene. However, she could certainly move fast on her hands and knees, and took a very dim view of my picking her up from the lawn so that while holding her, unknown to her I could pray a silent prayer for her needs to be met by God. She struggled to get down, so reluctantly I put her down, and she happily made her way on hands and knees among the bushes, intent upon some expedition of her own.

Shortly after this, I turned my head and saw her standing gazing into the blue sky; looking up I could see nothing else, and wondered at her private thoughts. There was immediately before her a tall, metal climbing apparatus, of the kind children love to play around, to climb on and over, and to turn and twist upon; in fact, what the experts have invented in a later generation than my own, and the sort of thing that fills grandparents with squeamish fears as their grandchildren learn acrobatics and doubtless strengthen their muscles and grip in the process. As a grandparent myself I could only barely accept the calm attitude of her parent in this case, but, of course, Nadine was as yet too tiny to climb and not strong enough to pull up her own weight, therefore her mother had no worry.

Then I saw something new to me. The child, standing on her one leg, holding with both hands the lowest rung of the metal frame while still gazing into the far distance, unconsciously raised the other leg straight up until it pointed heavenward, and began to rub the side of her head with the sole of her foot in a nonchalant way; I could not refrain a chuckle, and her mother looked round to see why, and said, 'Oh, we are used to that.'

'Well,' I quipped, 'there's one consolation; if she is not healed, she will always be able to earn her living on the stage!'

Later, I went indoors and chatted with her father, and then Nadine was carried in by her mother and dumped on the bed. She was an exhausted little girl by now; the heat and exertions of the afternoon had made their mark, along with the facial smudges of dirt collected in the serious matter of scrambling over the flower-beds. In a few minutes her eyes closed, and she slept soundly.

It was my opportunity, and I seized it, and as I placed my hands on her and prayed for God to speed up the growth of the hip socket—assuming one was forming according to nature, howbeit somewhat late—I had the silent, prayerful backing of her parents. Her father, I think, like many other vicars, had doubts about divine healing, but prayerfully hoped.

The summer and autumn went their way and winter began to make itself felt when next I heard of Nadine. I received a letter from her father which expressed concern that as yet things seemed to be just as before, and they were worried about the leg which, in spite of regular efforts by the doctors at a famous children's hospital whither this child had been taken at intervals from earliest age, was still out of place; each time the leg was put in place, it soon came out again.

I put the letter on one side as I felt uncertain what to do about it, but a few weeks later I felt the time had come to reply. Her father had said he wondered about my ministering again to Nadine, as 'offhand he couldn't recall anywhere in the New Testament where we were told to give the laying on of hands a second time'. If anyone had asked me about that five years ago I would not have had the answer, because I was then almost unaware of such a thing as divine healing. Now I wrote and reminded him of the occasion when Jesus ministered to a blind man who, when asked if he could see, answered excitedly: 'Yes, I can see men like trees, walking.' At which Jesus placed His hands on the man a second time, and then the man was enabled to see perfectly. If the Great Physician Himself had to lay on hands a second time, surely we imperfect followers of His could do so as often as we thought fit.

Nadine's father than rang and asked, as a result of prayer following my reply, if they could bring her to the Mission chapel so that I could minister to her there. Thus it was arranged for two days after Christmas. He explained on the phone that five weeks ago they had taken Nadine to the hospital again, and a new doctor took off the hip caliper she had been wearing in the hope that it would help to keep the limb in its socket. He threw the caliper on the bed, took one glance at the child and said: 'Well, that's all there is to it. The leg isn't in, so that's that.'

Her parents were aware of the fact, of course, as it is obvious to anyone when a leg is little more than an appendage. 'Surely,' they asked, 'you will put the caliper back on?' 'No, no, no!' he replied. 'She's had it on for the regulation period of nine months, and we never keep it on longer than that.' It seemed brusque, and as if the door of hope had closed. Maybe he sensed their hurt. 'I tell you what,' he said, 'bring her back six weeks from now, and we'll have another look.'

Five and a half weeks had passed since then, and on New Year's Day they had an appointment at the hospital. They did not know, but I had already heard from someone who knew them well that they had begun to wonder whether the child might never walk. Nevertheless, this only spurred them on to greater prayer, backed by the prayers of their church prayer group and other intercessors. For my part, I admit to some misgiving about this lively youngster being still long enough for me to pray over her when she arrived! I need not have worried.

Mother, Father, a nannie, and the older brother and sister arrived with Nadine punctually that December afternoon. Her father knelt on the cushion before the Lord's table, over which hangs the much-loved picture of Jesus with arms outstretched as if to say: 'Come unto me, all ye that travail and are heavy laden.' Nadine, so small beside him, knelt meekly enough. Inside the sanctuary I bent over and spoke to her: 'Nadine, I'm going to lay my hands on your head now, and ask Jesus to make your leg better so that you'll be able to walk.' She lifted her little face and said brightly, 'Yes, I know!'; so presumably she had been primed for the occasion.

She could not have been more still, and my doubts and fears fled, and as I began to pray I felt the presence of the Lord. Mother, Nannie and the other children sat on the front row of chairs, also silently praying. My own prayer was simple and brief: 'Heavenly Father, thank you for all you have done in answer to prayer made in August for the speeding up of the growth of this hip socket. Now I ask, in Jesus' name, that you will complete the growth of the socket if it is not already completed.' I hesitated a moment, then added quite firmly: 'And now, Lord, will you *please* put this leg into its socket once and for all, and see that it *never* comes out again! Thank you, Lord. Amen.'

I have heard authorities say one should never use the word 'Please' in praying, but then I'm not an authority. Sometimes I think our prayers are too often from the head and not the heart. Occasionally, a prayer may sound a little like an order, but one cannot order God to do anything. Nevertheless, my own brief prayer was said in no uncertain tones, and I don't think He minded! Standing back for a short time after resting my hand on Nadine's hip, I watched this two year old, who looked minute beside her praying father. There was peace in the chapel.

Rising, her father took her hand, and I took the other saying, 'Now, let's walk down the nave together.' Nadine was beaming with pleasure, her cheeks were flushed scarlet, her eyes shining with happiness. She could manage to walk, of course, so long as there was someone either side of her to hold her up. As we went she said with enthusiasm, 'I'm better now, Mummy, I'm really better!' This she repeated as we retraced our steps. We grown-ups all smiled, perhaps a little touched by her obvious assurance of faith, and as grown-ups will, we were moved to say, 'Bless her . . . dear little soul . . .' etc., but if there was a tinge of sadness in our words she wasn't aware of it. So they went their way. In four days she would be facing the doctors again. But it was Jesus, the lover of children, who once said, 'Out of the mouth of babes . . . cometh forth praise.'

On New Year's Day, on their return from the hospital, Nadine's father rang me. How changed the tone of his voice from the day I first met him at his bedside when he asked pointed questions about this and that regarding the healing ministry! Excitedly he told me how the doctor had taken one look at the child and said, 'Why, the leg is in its socket. This is wonderful!' Then he asked them to bring her back in a couple of months' time, for only time would tell whether it was going to remain in its socket permanently. Her father believed it would, for he said on the phone, 'I felt sure she would be healed. I would have been so disappointed if she were not, for I really believed she would.'

In fact, the leg never did come out of its socket again. When the return visit took place after the months had slipped by, Nadine was carefully examined, and x-rays were taken. I understand the doctors said there were two things about her case that interested them. They had never known a case in their experience where a hip socket had grown so fast. Moreover, it was now the exact measurement of the other hip socket!

For my part I ask myself, 'Who put the leg in its socket finally?' Her father said, 'What so impressed me was that the femur had thickened out at exactly the time the leg went into the socket, so it never came out again.' Maybe the medical men would agree that nature had brought it to its normal thickness. But then, I ask myself, 'What man has ever made a hip socket grow at such a fast rate?'

Her mother probably never asked any questions, for she had from the beginning a faith in a Jesus who heals today sometimes when men cannot. That was why, later, she turned up with all the children for a little service of thanksgiving in our chapel. 'I thought,' she said happily, 'you would like to share with us in Nadine's new leg!' which, if not exactly accurate, is just like a mother!

On my study mantelpiece I have a framed, enlarged

snapshot, a close-up of Nadine taken at Christmas when she was just three years old. How she had grown in that year since her healing! She is standing—(how wonderful to stand!)—at the kitchen sink, wearing what looks like a rubber pinafore, her hands concerned with washing dishes, and hers such an expressive face. On the back of the photograph her mother has written, 'With love from Nadine.' And has penned as an afterthought, 'Healed to serve.' What truth indeed, and from my own experience I can be sure that the child—who is in no way lame or crippled now—will find plenty of opportunity in a busy vicarage.

As I write this I hear from her father that Nadine, now not quite six years old, was the youngest taking part in a sponsored walk for Christian Aid—she walked twelve miles! Would we, her father said, praise God for 'great things He hath done'? We do indeed!

# 14　JIM

It was from Jim's friends that I first heard of him and his need. They were kindly Christians, members of a prayer group which had his and his family's interests at heart. They told me he was a policeman, and about a year ago had had a kidney removed because of cancer. Two years before, Jim had become a believing Christian, but now he was seriously ill at home and in much need of prayer, for his other kidney was also cancerous. Medically, there was no hope whatsoever for his recovery. So far as anyone knew he was not aware of his complaint, but his wife had been told he would live yet another six months. Hers was indeed a burden, but friends, relatives and neighbours lightened it whenever possible, and often popped in for a word with Jim.

His friends asked if I would go and minister to him, so I arranged to call at his home one afternoon at three o'clock. Not knowing the exact time of trains from London, I arrived at his home town at five minutes to three. It was a fifteen-minute walk to Jim's home. A gentleman who had already hired the only visible taxi at the station kindly agreed for me to ride with him, and so I rang the doorbell of Jim's home at precisely three o'clock. Just a small thing, but it somehow encouraged me, for I didn't wish to be late, and I'd wondered perhaps if Jim wasn't much used to clergy whether he might be apprehensive of my visit. This was an added reason for arriving punctually. A further reason was that his friends would link up with me in prayer at 3 p.m. though they were away on holiday.

His wife and I chatted a little while in the living room. Jim, I learned, was in bed in the lounge, which made things easier for his wife who was spared much running up and down stairs during the day. I discovered there was an only child, not yet thirteen years old, though when I saw her later she looked every bit of sixteen. Her mother said Mildred was a great comfort to her, for she could see her mother was concerned about Jim, and Mildred had a simple, childlike faith in Jesus' power to heal her father; moreover, she had asked Jesus to do so, surely that was sufficient. When I was asked if I would prefer to see Jim on my own, I said I would because he might want to say something about himself which he would not care to in his wife's presence. Moreover, a third person can sometimes with all the goodwill in the world say quite the wrong thing. For my part, I wished to make sure Jim was 'right' with Jesus.

Thinking about his physical condition on my way to visit him I felt a strange prompting to refer to death while talking with him. This is something so few wish for, and one cannot be too careful in speaking to those who in the natural have little likelihood of living very long. It wasn't that I had no faith in the Lord's power to raise Jim up, but an inner urging on the matter made me sensitive to the Spirit.

Soon I was closeted with Jim who was lying flat on his back, and he looked a bit worried. However, he explained that what troubled him was that he was often sick, and thought it might trouble me. No sooner had he mentioned it than he sat up and I held him for that purpose. I assured him that if young nurses can do it regularly in their nursing hours, why shouldn't I?—and that seemed to take his worry away.

I chatted awhile with him about himself, his wife and

daughter, and his garden. Then I spoke about divine healing and the Divine Physician. I was looking for an opening, knowing I must refer to death. Suddenly I seized an opportunity and in a chatty way said: 'It's awful being ill, and the enemy so often tells lies. A couple of years ago I found I had a lump and quite decided I had cancer! . . . I was scared for an hour or two, and then suddenly pulled myself together. After all, we have to go sometime—though of course you're years younger than me so I suppose I'll go long before you!—and I sharply told myself I was supposed to be a Christian! Didn't Jesus say, "I go to prepare a place for you . . .", and wasn't that going to be for everyone who believed in Him as Saviour?—a place exactly right at the right time? And d'you know, Jim, from that moment I lost all my fears of cancer and dying. And, of course, the enemy had been lying.'

Then I abruptly changed the conversation and led him to hand over any sins to the Lord, seeing that we don't want them, nor do our friends or relatives want them, and anyway, Jesus has already paid the penalty for them. And Jim did so, and I absolved him. I rather think I explained anointing for healing (cf. Jas. 5:14) and then obeyed the scriptural injunction: so ended my ministry.

Finally, standing back from the bed I looked down on this man who was just over forty years of age. He lay quite still, eyes closed. And then I had a strange thought —more than that, a compelling of the Spirit. I felt I should kiss him.

This at once became a challenge. One doesn't normally go round in the ministry kissing one's patients, least of all a policeman! Yet, I tried to reason, if I do such a thing Jim will think I'm mad. Then came the thought almost as if spoken: if you don't, you'll always regret it.

Maybe the Holy Spirit gave me a push; I dropped to my knees beside him, leaned over and gently kissed his forehead. Doubtless with astonishment, his eyes flashed toward me; I said: 'That, Jim, was the kiss of peace . . . as from Jesus.' In a moment I was up on my feet. I picked up my Bible, saying: 'Now I'm going to have that cup of tea your wife has for me.' So I left him.

His wife indeed gave me a cup of tea, and we chatted for a time and then Mildred came in and joined us, for she had been shopping.

Shortly after, I called out, 'Cheerio!' to Jim as I left the house, but did not go in to see him, and his tone of voice when he answered strongly 'Goodbye' was such that it made me feel he was happy about my visit.

Ten days later I had a letter from Jim's wife. I had been to see him on a Thursday, and I could recall walking back to the station saying in prayer, 'Father, you know all about Jim. You can heal that kidney of cancer, you can even create one in place of the missing one. But somehow, Father, I don't think you will. I don't lack faith, nor do I wish to be negative, but, Father, I've a feeling he is not going to recover. If this be so, then please don't let him linger for six months in distress and maybe fear. Moreover, his wife doesn't look very strong, and it won't be easy nursing him, to say nothing of the emotional stress that will go with it, and in the end it will seem of no avail. So Father, heal him . . . or take him, but spare them both unnecessary suffering.'

The letter from Jim's wife moved me. On the Saturday morning, barely nine days after my visit, Jim was resting quietly in his bed. His wife and Mildred were with him. Jim said to Mildred: 'Go and play my favourite piece of music for me, love.'

'All right, Dad,' she said; and happily went to the piano in the other room, leaving the door open so he could enjoy it. Her mother sat beside Jim as he closed his eyes and listened, but before Mildred had played through her father's favourite piece of music he had slipped away to be with the Lord: quietly, so unexpectedly, so peacefully. The shock was great; but now Jim's wife wrote of the doctor's astonishment, and how another doctor was called in because Jim's passing six months earlier than expected had to be explained.

In her letter she asked me what I had said or done for Jim; for from the time of my visit, without exception and without any word from her to the frequent callers who had come to see him, each one had said much the same thing: 'What's happened to Jim? He's so peaceful, so changed.' His wife wrote: 'I would not call it a surrender, but a kind of acceptance.'

That night Mildred slept upstairs with her mother, and not unnaturally their sleep was somewhat disturbed. Next morning Mildred said: 'Mother, I was scared during the night.' And when her mother asked why, Mildred said: 'Well, I heard Dad call me as clear as anything, and I know it was his voice. He called me by name, twice.'

Her mother asked her what he had said, and she replied 'He said, "Mildred! Mildred! Be a good girl . . . and look after your mother." '

At Mildred's age, amid the disappointment and sorrow of seemingly unanswered prayer, surely the Lord had graciously permitted Jim to say a word clearly to her. It is so easy for the enemy to rob the young of their faith; but now Mildred knows her father is alive! Mother and daughter were grateful that Jim had been spared months of pain and distress. For my part, I firmly believe Jim's place in the Church in Paradise was ready for him.

'Blessed are they who die in the Lord.'

Surely, Jim's healing was the best healing of all.

## 15 CONCLUSION

As I write this last chapter Lucy and I can look back through nine years of experience in the healing ministry. Not long, perhaps, but in that time we have learnt much, not least from others who have written books about the subject of divine healing, some of whom have personally shared with us what they have gleaned from their experience. To them, and to all who have worked with us in our ministry, as well as to the very many who have upheld us in their prayers, I would express our warm appreciation. The stories you have read involved people too numerous to mention by name, not least those on the staffs both in Natal and London. Through our 'venture into healing' all have had a share in its results, for under God many have not only been healed of sickness of body or mind, but have now a deeper measure of faith in Him through Jesus Christ whom they have come to know as Saviour as well as Healer. To Him be all the praise!

The purpose of this book as expressed in its Preface has, I hope, been fulfilled. I did not feel led—or competent—to write about the problems raised concerning the subject of divine healing. Indeed, others far better qualified have already written books to deal with them. I have, however, been asked to add something for those who are not healed, those who sometimes have great faith in God and His power to heal, yet remain unhealed physically. We all ask questions—like the first disciples of Jesus, but He didn't always answer them! Perhaps it is not necessary for us to know all the answers. Maybe we never shall in this life. My own conclusion is that no one of us in this ministry—nor even all of us put together —have satisfactory answers to all the questions.

Be that as it may, from the time of my ordination when I first began visiting the sick—without then having any knowledge of divine healing outside the Bible stories —there were occasional experiences when the Lord's redemptive power reached out and touched me through the sublime courage and faith of some sufferers. God had not healed them physically, but He had redeemed their suffering and pain so that my own poor quality of life was put to shame. I did not help them, they helped me.

In the course of my work I still occasionally come across those who are confined to the narrow limits of their bed, which they never leave. Their little room or hospital ward is their world, and it is there that they live out their lives. God has given them a grace to keep faith in Him. They don't ask questions, perhaps because long ago they concluded it was a waste of time and energy. They have accepted their lot. One cannot but admire the cheerfulness some retain in spite of it. Among them are some who really love the Lord. Their witness is ever a challenge to those who both wait on them and visit them.

Yet, having admitted all this, I sometimes ask if they have ever heard about divine healing. It seems most have not. So even those who have faith in God for other things may never have had faith for their healing. They were never told to believe for it, or to claim it on God's promises.

My mind goes back to the visit of Jesus to such people lying around the Pool of Bethesda. Very few of them really expected healing . . . the medical men had given their verdict: 'Incurable!'. Jesus approached a man who had been crippled for thirty-eight years. How oddly His question falls upon our ears: 'Do you want to be well?' Yet there are many people in the East today who only survive because of their deformities; to be healed of them means they would get nothing by begging, and as likely starve. Not least is this still tragically true for some victims of leprosy.

But what of people in the West? In my ministry I frequently come across those who will make no effort to build up faith in a healing Christ. They trot around to every 'healer' in turn! They prefer to be sick—and talk of nothing else. Indeed, they are sick because they think only of themselves. Many such may end up in the wards of our psychiatric hospitals. Then there are countless others who are sick simply because they ignore the simple rules of health for body, for mind, and for soul. Even after divine healing one must keep to the rules of health.

The task of the Church as I see it is to obey the Lord's command: 'Heal the sick'. He has commissioned us for this in the way He commissioned His first disciples. As in my case, they had no medical knowledge or training. They most certainly would never have thought they would be used some day to heal the sick. That they did so is irrefutable. Moreover, for a few centuries the healing work of the Church continued; it was not just reserved, as some would suggest, for the thirty-five years briefly covered by the Acts of the Apostles. When eventually men compromised with the Word of God their faith dwindled correspondingly. This is a lesson to us. For some fourteen centuries or more the clergy went about their pastoral work and left the healing side of it largely to the monks in their monasteries. They, at least, would provide some practical help, provide herbal medicines and bind up open wounds, as well as pray.

Now, in our twentieth century, the healing ministry has revived. It should in no way cut across the work of qualified medical men. Rather do I visualise our respective work as furrows running parallel like those in a ploughed field, a common end in view which spells eventual health. Neither can yield a harvest apart from God who works always according to the laws He invented.

The plain fact is that the Power of the Holy Spirit and the Authority of Jesus Christ have never been withdrawn from His Church, only ignored for far too long a time. It is all to the good that in our own century the Church's healing ministry is being increasingly practised. We owe a considerable debt under God to those who pioneered its revival.

Recently I attended a conference on exorcism. Seven clergy among us had been requested to attend by their diocesan bishop. Ordinands training for their ministry in the Church would be better equipped for their work if they were taught and trained for that part of it which involves divine healing. At the same time, the guide-lines laid down in the New Testament Church should be carefully adhered to. Our task is to bring men and women to Jesus Christ for the wholeness He alone can bestow. The Word of God and the example of Jesus nowhere suggest we may achieve that by dabbling with things of the psychic realm or the occult. Moreover, that is extremely dangerous. I would stress here the danger of exposing oneself to evil powers. Let no one try an exorcism unless he has been called to that part of the healing ministry, and been at least taught, if not trained, for such a task by men well qualified to do so. Many have suffered from the rebound because they did not know how to protect themselves from enemy action.

It is wonderful to receive, as many are doing nowadays, the fulness of the Holy Spirit. Yet this does not give them automatically or necessarily a 'ministry' of healing or indeed of exorcism. Young people should be warned that if we invade enemy territory we can expect a battle, and in this case ignorance—with all the good intentions in the world—will not save them from possible dire consequences. I have seen sufficient evidence to justify this warning. The Lord Himself will make it known to us individually when He is leading us into this kind of ministry. Until He does, no one should attempt a 'deliverance ministry'.

I would re-emphasise the spiritual foundation of our healing work. Our Lord's wonderful ministry of healing was due to His perfect relationship with the Father. It was based on a completely yielded will and a life of utter dedication and prayer. By His grace we must so live as to be clean channels of His healing love. That love never ceases toward us. He loves us not because of our sins but in spite of them. He loves us not because of our sicknesses but in spite of them. Those who are healed should use their health to serve others, and testify to God's love. Those who are laid aside in sickness have the opportunity to seek God's face. Some do, and so are healed. Others do, but remain bedfast. Such should never cease to expect divine healing, for God's revealed will is health for all of us. If it is not, then we have no right whatsoever to go to a doctor for healing! The mystery remains. Yet Christ does not withdraw His presence from the unhealed.

Many more are needed in this ministry. It may well be that among those who have read this book are some who the Lord will move to undertake as we did a 'venture into healing'. That is our prayer.

All royalties from the sale of this book
will be donated to

The London Healing Mission
20 Dawson Place
London W2 4TL

ANALYZING ENVIRONMENTAL CHANGE

# ANALYZING
# THREATS TO
# WATER RESOURCES

## ASKING QUESTIONS, EVALUATING EVIDENCE,
## AND DESIGNING SOLUTIONS

PHILIP STEELE

Cavendish
Square

New York

Published in 2019 by Cavendish Square
Publishing, LLC, 243 5th Avenue, Suite 136,
New York, NY 10016

Copyright © 2017 Wayland, a division of
Hachette Children's Group

First Edition

Website: cavendishsq.com

This publication represents the opinions
and views of the author based on his or her
personal experience, knowledge, and
research. The information in this book serves
as a general guide only. The author and
publisher have used their best efforts in
preparing this book and disclaim liability
rising directly or indirectly from the use
and application of this book.

All websites were available and accurate
when this book was sent to press.

Cataloging-in-Publication Data

Names: Steele, Philip.
Title: Analyzing threats to water resources:
asking questions, evaluating evidence, and
designing solutions / Philip Steele.
Description: New York : Cavendish Square,
2019. | Series: Analyzing environmental
change | Includes glossary and index.
Identifiers: ISBN 9781502639325 (library
bound) | ISBN 9781502639332 (pbk.) |
ISBN 9781502639349 (ebook)
Subjects: LCSH: Water conservation--
Juvenile literature. | Water-supply--Juvenile
literature. | Water pollution--Juvenile
literature. | Environmental protection--
Juvenile literature.
Classification: LCC TD388.S834 2019 |
DDC 333.91--dc23

Produced for Cavendish Square by
Tall Tree Ltd
Editors: Jon Richards
Designers: Ed Simkins

Printed in the United States of America

# CONTENTS

# IT'S TIME TO TALK ABOUT
# WATER

It has no color. It has no smell. Even though we use water every day, we hardly give it a thought. Yet it is water that keeps us and our world alive. Without it we could not exist.

## SHAPING OUR PLANET

Seen from space, our planet looks blue, with patches of white cloud. Salty oceans cover about 70 percent of Earth's surface. Water has shaped our rocks, our valleys and hills, our coasts and soils over billions of years.

People struggle to travel through flooded streets in Thailand. Monsoon rains cause flooding in many parts of southern Asia every year.

"Water is good. It benefits all things..."

Laozi, Chinese philosopher, c. 604-531 BCE

# WATER IS LIFE

Life on Earth began in the water, sometime between 4.2 and 3.5 billion years ago. Then, around 445 million years ago, all sorts of life forms evolved in water and slowly began to move on to land.

Our climate on Earth is created by water and by the Sun. The amount of rainfall determines the plant and animal life in any one region. Water and climate influence every aspect of human life. They affect population numbers, where and how we live, our health, our farming and food, our energy and industry.

## FLOODWATERS

A large proportion of the world's population lives on or close to the coast. Strong rains and tides can cause devastating floods.

## HYDROELECTRICITY

Flowing water has been used for thousands of years to power mills and factories. Today, we build huge dams, such as the Pak Mun Dam in Thailand (above), which convert the flow of water to produce electricity.

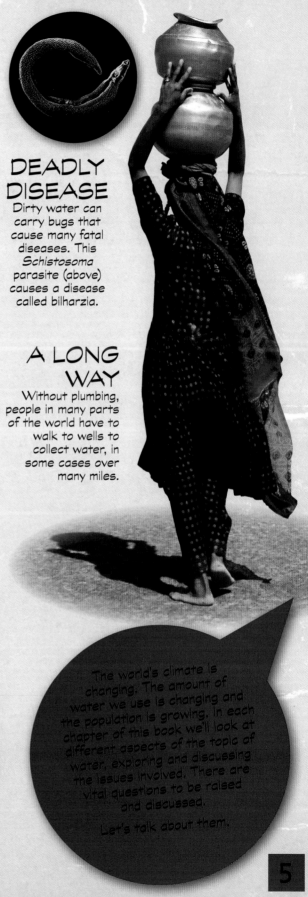

## DEADLY DISEASE

Dirty water can carry bugs that cause many fatal diseases. This *Schistosoma* parasite (above) causes a disease called bilharzia.

## A LONG WAY

Without plumbing, people in many parts of the world have to walk to wells to collect water, in some cases over many miles.

The world's climate is changing. The amount of water we use is changing and the population is growing. In each chapter of this book we'll look at different aspects of the topic of water, exploring and discussing the issues involved. There are vital questions to be raised and discussed.

Let's talk about them.

# SO, WHAT IS WATER?

The chemical formula is $H_2O$. This means that each molecule of water binds one oxygen atom together with two hydrogen atoms. Water exists as a liquid, but also as a solid (ice) and as a gas (water vapor). Many minerals and other substances dissolve in water, such as the salts found in seawater. Water with a very low level of salts or other dissolved solids is called fresh water. We use fresh water for drinking, washing, cooking and watering plants.

## FRESH WATER SOURCES

Fresh water makes up less than 3 percent of all the water on our planet. Much of that is deep frozen all year round in the ice caps surrounding the North and South Poles. We can only access a tiny amount of fresh water, less than 0.01 percent of the total, from lakes and rivers. More fresh water can be found underground.

0.01% accessible

3% fresh water

97% salt water

# WHY DO WE NEED IT?

Humans need to drink water to stay alive. A healthy adult living in a mild climate needs at least 1.5 liters during the course of a day. Our blood and our body tissues contain water and water forms part of the body's natural chemical processes, such as digesting food. Water brings nutrients from food to our body cells, while urine carries away unwanted waste. Water helps to regulate our body temperature, for example when we sweat. It also protects parts of the body from knocks and helps our joints to move smoothly.

Up to 65%

90%

## NUMBER CRUNCH

50 to 65 percent of an adult's body is made up of water. Our brains are about 90 percent water!

# THE WATER CYCLE

Water is finite. There is only so much of it to go around, and we cannot make any more of it. The water on the planet is in endless motion, part of a cycle created by the warmth of the Sun.

## HOW DOES THE WATER CYCLE WORK?

### THREE STATES
The temperature range on Earth means that water can exist in its three states — liquid water, solid ice and gassy water vapor.

**3** As the water vapor rises, it cools. This turns it back into tiny droplets of liquid water, which form clouds, fog or mist in the air.

**2** As a warm gas, the water vapor rises into the atmosphere.

**1** The liquid water on the Earth's surface evaporates or turns into vapor when heated by the Sun.

In the sea, the water evaporates and the cycle begins all over again. **7**

# FOR GOOD OR FOR BAD

Human progress has always depended on the water cycle, but it has often cost us dearly. For thousands of years people have settled near rivers, where there is plenty of water for drinking and irrigating crops. Along the banks of the Yellow River in China, flooding left behind a rich muddy soil where crops would grow well. However, over the ages the same floods have also killed many millions of people. Humans have always battled to control and manage water as well as use it.

**4** As droplets collect together, they become heavy. They fall to the ground as rain, or in frozen forms such as hail, snow or sleet. This is called precipitation.

**5** In some places, the rainwater collects to form lakes or underground water stores.

**6** The rainwater may bubble up as springs. Rain may also run off directly into streams and rivers, and flow down to the sea.

"Water is the driving force of all nature."

Leonardo da Vinci, Italian artist, sculptor, inventor and engineer, 1452-1519

# TURN ON THE TAP

Water needs to be collected and stored. On a small scale, rainwater may be collected in butts, cisterns or tanks and used by a single household or a village. Modern towns and cities in the developed world are served by huge reservoirs. These can be formed by rivers or lakes that have been dammed to collect the water.

The Hoover Dam lies between the US states of Nevada and Arizona. It holds back the waters of Lake Mead, the largest reservoir by volume in the US.

## CLEANING WATER

Reservoir water must be processed at a special plant before it can be used. Particles in the water settle and any twigs or leaves are screened out. The water is then filtered through layers of coarse and fine sand. Chemicals such as chlorine or hypochlorites are added to kill off any bacteria and other microbes that could make people ill.

# PIPED TO THE HOME

The water is then piped and pumped along water mains to each building. Here it may be used in central heating radiators or released through hot or cold taps for use in bathrooms, kitchens or washing machines. Few things have changed people's everyday lives as much as easy access to water.

## EASY ACCESS

Many wealthy countries can afford to build large and complicated systems that deliver water right into your home when you turn on a tap.

## LET'S DISCUSS...
## MAINS WATER

US

380

Average consumption per person per day (liters)

Recommended (UN figures)

50

Africa
20

• is clean and good for public health.

• is convenient and accessible.

• can be recycled and used again.

• encourages people to use much more water than they need.

• needs expensive maintenance and repair.

• is not available in many parts of the world.

# WATER FROM THE WELL

In the more developed parts of the world, about 87 percent of people can get clean, treated water straight from the bathroom tap. But elsewhere it's a different story. One third of the world's population – that's about 2.5 billion people – have no water piped to their homes.

## NATURAL SOURCES

Instead, they have to collect their water from natural sources, such as springs, rivers or wells. Dig deep into the ground in many places and you will probably reach some water. Even under the world's largest hot desert, the Sahara, there are underground reserves of water.

This oasis, surrounded by sand dunes, lies in the Ica region of southern Peru, close to the Pacific Ocean.

## GROUND WATER

Rocks, gravel and sand that soak up or trap rainwater underground are called aquifers. The level to which the ground is saturated is called the water table. Digging a deep well by hand can be dangerous. Modern drilling is much safer, but expensive. Engineers drill down to reach the aquifer. If the water is under pressure from the surrounding rocks it may rise to the surface naturally. If not, it will need to be pumped.

# A LONG WALK

Wells are often far from a village, and people have to walk for hours each day carrying heavy containers of water. It is tiring and takes up time that could be spent at school or farming the land. One clever invention has been the plastic water drum, which can be pulled along the ground. People in dry and remote areas need new wells, but there may not be enough water to go around. The supply needs to be sustainable.

## FETCH AND CARRY
These women are collecting water from a well in the Indian town of Vasai, close to Mumbai, India.

In Africa, only 4 percent of available water resources can be accessed, because of the lack of wells, pipes, pumps and reservoirs.

4%

| 1 liter | 1 liter | 1 liter | 1 liter | 1 liter |
|---|---|---|---|---|
| 1 liter | 1 liter | 1 liter | 1 liter | 1 liter |

In some developing countries, each person on average uses only 10 liters of water a day (see page 11).

## LET'S DISCUSS...
# WATER FROM WELLS

- keeps people alive in remote areas.
- allows people to water their crops.
- can now be pumped using solar power.

- will run dry when the aquifer is used up.
- has to be fetched and carried.
- may become contaminated or dirty.

13

# WATER
## FROM THE SEA

If we could drink the water from the ocean, we could solve all our water shortages. But we can't, at least not very easily. Seawater is salty and drinking it makes us sick. Some inland water in rivers and lakes is also a bit too salty, or brackish. Salt water is not good for irrigation either, as it destroys crops.

## FILTERING

Taking the salt out of seawater is called desalination. Various industrial processes can be used. One method is called reverse osmosis. This screens and filters the seawater and then pumps it through spiral membranes under very high pressure. Typically, every two liters of seawater can produce one liter of fresh water.

## REVERSE OSMOSIS
These tubes are using special sheets, or membranes, to remove tiny particles from water using reverse osmosis, making it suitable for drinking.

# DESALINATION

In recent years, the technology used for large-scale desalination has become a lot smarter. Desalination is now being used in 120 countries, including Saudi Arabia and Spain. This way of accessing water is likely to grow in the future in regions where there is little rainfall and a high risk of drought.

On a small scale, pots or homemade desalination kits can be used to produce water for a single household. Water in a container is heated or warmed by the sun. The liquid water turns into vapor, leaving behind salts and any other particles. The vapor passes through a tube into a cool container, where it condenses into drinkable water. This process is called distilling.

This large-scale desalination plant lies on the coast of the Spanish island of Lanzarote in the Atlantic Ocean.

In every gallon (3.8 L) of seawater there are about 4.5 ounces (128 g) of dissolved salts.

## LET'S DISCUSS...
## LARGE-SCALE DESALINATION

• accesses the world's biggest source of water.

• saves using up existing fresh water sources.

• uses much improved technology.

• has to be located on coasts or islands.

• is expensive to install.

• leaves behind highly concentrated brine and other contaminants.

# ENDING POVERTY

According to the United Nations, by 2025, 1.8 billion people in the world will be living in regions where there will be a severe shortage of water. Who will be hit the hardest? The world's poorest countries.

A boy collects dirty water from a well in Uganda, Africa.

## QUESTION IT!
## IS ACCESSING WATER THE BEST WAY TO END POVERTY?

**WITHOUT GOOD ACCESS TO WATER** it is hard to organize farming, healthcare, education or new industries. Water poverty means economic poverty.

**POOR FARMERS OR HERDERS CANNOT AFFORD TO DRILL** and maintain new wells. That is why many international organizations fund the building of new wells in regions at risk from drought.

**WATER IS NOT DISTRIBUTED** in even quantities around the world. Sixty percent of the world's people who live in lands that have a shortage of water are unable to grow enough crops for their food.

**NEW WELLS MAY NOT ALWAYS BE THE ANSWER.** They may be hard or too expensive to maintain. They may take too much water from aquifers. They may encourage people to live in places that are not sustainable in the long term, and so prolong poverty.

**WATER SHORTAGE IS JUST ONE OF MANY REASONS FOR POVERTY.** Unfair trade agreements, corruption, bad government and warfare all prevent development. The wider political problems also need sorting out in order to defeat poverty.

17

# THE HEAT IS ON

Weather is what we experience every day, come rain or shine. Climate is the pattern of weather in any given place over a longer period, such as 30 years or more. Water plays a key role in the global climate system.

This painting shows people skating on the frozen canals of Rotterdam, the Netherlands, in 1825. It is thought that winters were more severe at that time.

## COOLING AND WARMING

Of course the climate can change. It has always done so. In the past, Earth has been gripped by ice ages, and has warmed during the periods in between, known as interglacials. At the moment Earth should be cooling, but it's not. It's cooking. World temperatures began to rise during the factory age of the 1800s, and they are now soaring. Is that due to a natural variability in our climate? More than 97 percent of scientists think not. They have found that climate change has very likely been created by human activities.

# CAUSING THE GREENHOUSE EFFECT

Many people blame gases such as carbon dioxide ($CO_2$). These are pumped out into the atmosphere by factory chimneys, forest fires, planes, cars and construction sites. They collect in the atmosphere. As heat from the Sun is reflected back from Earth's surface, it is trapped by these greenhouse gases and bounced back again. This reflected heat warms the atmosphere even more, disrupting weather patterns and melting ice caps.

## GREENHOUSE GASES

Many people believe that polluting gases from car exhausts and factories are responsible for increasing the greenhouse effect.

## NUMBER CRUNCH

The surface temperature of Earth's land and oceans has risen by about 1.53°F (0.85°C) since 1880.

## LET'S DISCUSS...
## CARBON DIOXIDE

- is part of the natural cycle of life on Earth.
- is absorbed by the oceans in large quantities.
- is absorbed by the world's great rain forests.

- is one of the gases overheating our planet.
- is making the oceans more acidic.
- is increasing as the world's forests are being destroyed.

# 2 WILD WATER, DRY LAND

WATER AND CLIMATE

Human activities have often created problems with water in the past. Overgrazing or intensive farming sometimes destroy the vegetation and roots that trap moisture in the soil, turning land into desert or a dust bowl. If people cut down trees in river valleys, the soil erodes, and this can cause disastrous flooding downstream.

## DROUGHT AND FLOODS

Scientists predict that human-made climate change will bring a new age of drought, floods and extreme storms. Indeed, it is already happening. In a warmer world, the air heats up and expands, and it can hold more water vapor for rain. The effects of climate change are hard to predict. Different regions may be affected in very different ways, or suffer more because of natural variations. These include the El Niño climate cycle in the Pacific, which causes extreme flooding and drought on opposite sides of the planet.

### WILD WEATHER
As more and more energy is released into the atmosphere, we may see an increase in severe weather events, such as hurricanes.

Prolonged dry periods, known as droughts, cause the ground to dry out and crack, and crops cannot grow in it.

## CHANGING PATTERNS

In places that have often had droughts in the past, the periods of intense heat without rain are becoming longer and more extreme. The old climate patterns have changed, so nobody is sure when to plant crops now. Even when rain does come, it may flood the hard, baked soil. Have humans turned water, their best friend, into their own worst enemy?

## EXTREME DROUGHT

Animal bones litter the ground in the Kruger National Park, South Africa. Prolonged drought threatens water supplies for people and animals.

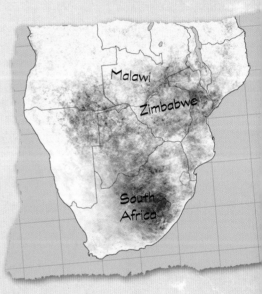

Malawi

Zimbabwe

South Africa

## NUMBER CRUNCH

A long drought in southern Africa, associated with El Niño, is threatening food supplies and public health. The map on the right shows how temperatures increased between 2000 and 2015. The red areas represent areas that were hotter than usual during this period. By 2016, about 14 million people were being affected in countries such as Malawi, Zimbabwe and South Africa.

## THINK ABOUT...
## CLIMATE CHANGE

- increases water shortages in many regions.
- increases the danger of flooding in others.
- makes extreme storms more likely.

21

# TROUBLE AT SEA

The oceans are the great engines of our climate. Currents of cold or warm water circulate between the Equator and the Poles. One of them, called the North Atlantic Drift, warms the shores of northwest Europe and gives the region a mild climate. Seasonal monsoons carry water from the Indian Ocean to fall in torrents of rain on the parched lands of southern Asia.

With less sea ice to hunt on in the Arctic, polar bears find it harder to catch food, and have to travel farther and farther to get enough to survive.

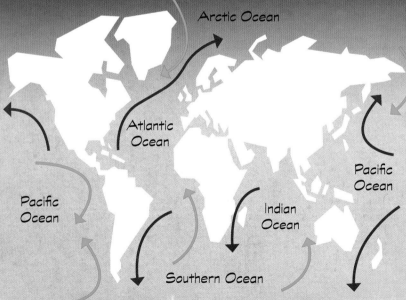

Arctic Ocean

Atlantic Ocean

Pacific Ocean

Pacific Ocean

Indian Ocean

Southern Ocean

## SWIRLING CURRENTS

This map shows the main ocean currents carrying warm (red) and cold (blue) water around the globe.

## SEA CHANGE

When it comes to global warming, the oceans do us a favor, because they naturally absorb a lot of the problematic carbon dioxide. The trouble is, the $CO_2$ levels in the ocean are now so high that they are making the seawater acidic. This damages all sorts of marine habitats, such as coral reefs. The oceans also expand as they warm. This makes sea levels rise, so that they flood lowlands and islands. On coral islands in the Pacific Ocean, rising saltwater can soak into freshwater aquifers, making wells unusable.

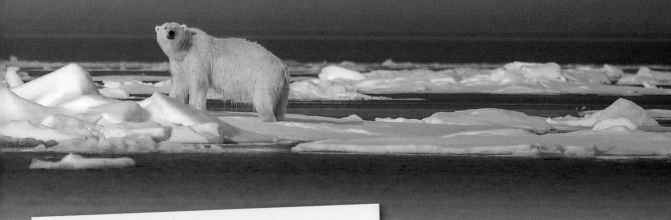

## NUMBER CRUNCH

About 23 percent of the world's population lives on or near the coast. Sea level rises will present a huge problem.

# ARCTIC MELT

Sea levels also rise because much of the polar ice is melting. The Arctic sea ice has shrunk by 20 percent since 1979. Part of the East Antarctic ice sheet has actually been growing, probably because of a natural current switch in the Pacific Ocean. Sea levels are expected to carry on rising for a long time, even if we cut down on $CO_2$ emissions now.

## FLOOD DEFENSES

These flood defences in the Netherlands are designed to hold back rising sea levels. However, they are expensive to construct and not every country can afford to build them.

## THINK ABOUT... THE ARCTIC

- The tundra is melting, releasing more greenhouse gases.
- More shipping as sea ice melts means even more carbon emissions.
- Melting ice is raising sea levels.

# TACKLING CLIMATE CHANGE

In 1992, the United Nations held the first Earth Summit in Rio de Janeiro, Brazil. Since then, policies have been agreed upon to deal with water shortages, storms and floods caused by or made worse by climate change. But are they going to work?

## QUESTION IT!

## ARE WE DOING ENOUGH TO TACKLE CLIMATE CHANGE?

**THE PARIS SUMMIT IN 2015** set a target of limiting the increase in global warming to under 3.6°F (2°C). Some scientists predict that this could result in zero carbon emissions by the middle of this century.

**GREEN MEASURES** include planting new forests to soak up more carbon dioxide, and preventing forests being cut down. In recent decades, forests have absorbed 30 percent of global $CO_2$ emissions.

## NUMBER CRUNCH

Water shortages, made worse by climate change, could reduce the ability of countries to create wealth — their gross domestic product or GDP — by 6 percent.

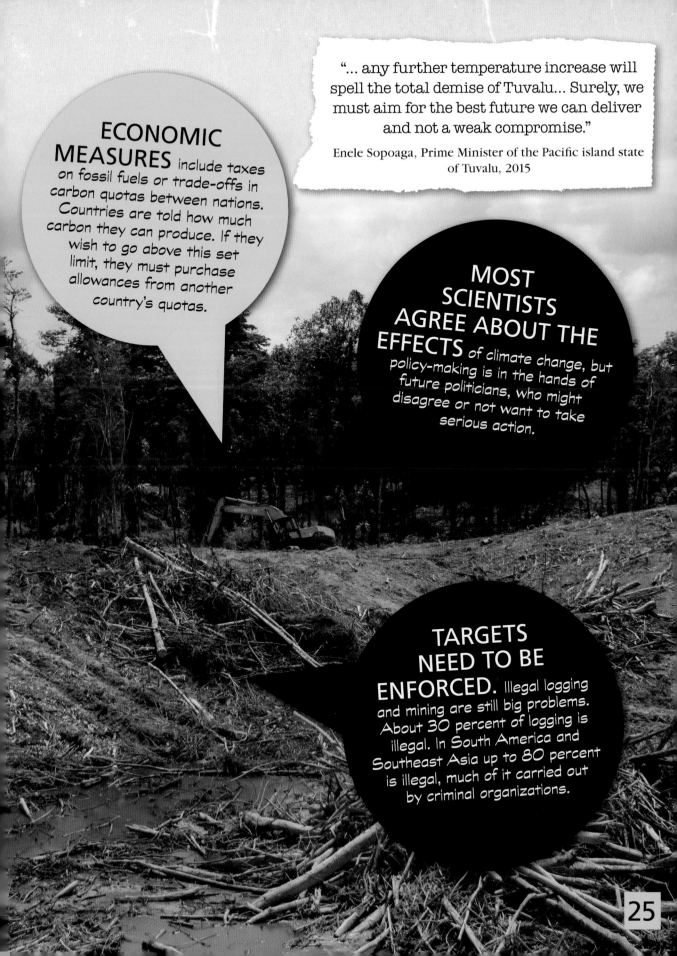

ECONOMIC MEASURES include taxes on fossil fuels or trade-offs in carbon quotas between nations. Countries are told how much carbon they can produce. If they wish to go above this set limit, they must purchase allowances from another country's quotas.

"... any further temperature increase will spell the total demise of Tuvalu... Surely, we must aim for the best future we can deliver and not a weak compromise."

Enele Sopoaga, Prime Minister of the Pacific island state of Tuvalu, 2015

MOST SCIENTISTS AGREE ABOUT THE EFFECTS of climate change, but policy-making is in the hands of future politicians, who might disagree or not want to take serious action.

TARGETS NEED TO BE ENFORCED. Illegal logging and mining are still big problems. About 30 percent of logging is illegal. In South America and Southeast Asia up to 80 percent is illegal, much of it carried out by criminal organizations.

# WATER AND HEALTH

We all think of water as something clean that keeps us alive. But for many people in the world, water is unhealthy and even a threat to life itself. About 3.5 million people are thought to die each year from diseases caused by drinking, washing or cooking with contaminated water.

## IS IT SAFE?

In some parts of the world, the same source of water is used for cleaning, washing, drinking, cooking and even as a toilet.

## POOR ACCESS

About 2.5 billion people in the world have no access to proper toilets or drainage. They mostly live in remote country areas, or in city slums. Human or animal waste may seep into rivers or ground water and contaminate wells. A supply of safe, clean water is one of the greatest needs around the world.

About 783 million people in the world do not have access to clean water - that's more than one in ten.

## NUMBER CRUNCH

These children in the Indian city of Mumbai are learning how washing and personal hygiene help to prevent the spread of diseases.

# WATERBORNE DISEASES

Water may be the breeding ground for insects such as mosquito larvae. A parasite from some mosquito species spreads deadly malaria, which killed about 438,000 people in 2015. Other diseases carried by water include cholera and dysentery. These were once common in cities such as London and Paris, until proper sewers and water systems were constructed in the 1860s. Sanitation is essential for public health. Money is also well spent on education – teaching children the importance of washing their hands or boiling water to make it safe.

## LET'S DISCUSS... CLEAN WATER SUPPLIES

- are being installed in many parts of the world.
- prevent all sorts of diseases.
- save money on hospitals and healthcare.

- are still not available to millions of people.
- are expensive to install.
- must be protected against pollution.

27

# POLLUTION PERIL

All sorts of industrial chemicals, detergents, pesticides, metals and household garbage find their way into lakes, rivers and oceans. They pollute the water and threaten the health of plants, animals and humans.

## RIVERS THAT DIED

Rain washes nitrogen from fertilizers used on farmland into rivers and estuaries such as the Mississippi Delta. This reduces the levels of oxygen that support life, so a whole food chain is soon destroyed and huge areas become 'dead zones.'
In the 1960s, the Cuyahoga River, in Ohio, became so polluted that it caught fire. New clean river laws were passed there and in many other countries, but they are not always enforced. One of the most polluted rivers is the Citarum, in Java, Indonesia, which is massively poisoned with lead.

Waste clogs up a river in the southern Indian state of Tamil Nadu.

"We know that when we protect our oceans we're protecting our future."

Bill Clinton, 42nd US President

# THE TOXIC OCEANS

The pollution of the oceans can be just as bad. A spill from the *Deepwater Horizon* oil rig in the Gulf of Mexico in 2010 released 4.6 million barrels of sticky black oil into the sea. It killed fish and birds, affected the tourism and fishing industries and exposed humans to toxins. A major disaster at the Fukushima Daiichi nuclear complex in Japan poured radioactive water into the Pacific Ocean in 2011, and is still doing so more than five years later.

## RAGING FIRE
The fire on the *Deepwater Horizon* led to the largest oil spill is US waters.

## MICROPLASTICS
Microplastics, such as these fibers, are tiny pieces of plastic that are smaller than 0.2 inches (5 mm). They are used in a wide range of products, such as cosmetics, and enter the environment during industrial processes or when we wash ourselves.

The world's oceans are filling up with plastic. As well as debris, there are tiny particles of industrial plastic. In the Pacific Ocean, these have formed a gigantic floating garbage patch. They are swallowed by fish and marine mammals. Polluting water means poisoning the planet's life-support system.

## LET'S DISCUSS... TACKLING POLLUTION

- New laws have cleaned up cities.
- Fish soon return to rivers that have been cleaned up.
- International laws now prevent dumping at sea.

- Clearing up an oil spill can cost billions of dollars.
- Oil companies still want to drill in the Arctic Ocean.
- Noise made by humans and machines can also harm marine creatures.

29

# RAIN FORESTS THREATENED

The Amazon drains about 2.7 million square miles (7 million square km) of tropical land and pours 55 million gallons (209 million L) of water into the Atlantic Ocean every second. Its rain forest has been under attack from illegal loggers and ranchers. In places, miners have poisoned its precious water.

## QUESTION IT!

## SHOULD WE BLAME ILLEGAL GOLD MINERS FOR POISONING THE AMAZON?

SOME 30,000 MINERS FIRST CAME TO THE PERUVIAN part of the forest in the 1980s, to pan the rivers.

### NUMBER CRUNCH

The Amazon delivers about 25 percent of all the fresh water flowing into the oceans.

### BEFORE AND AFTER

These two satellite images taken in 2003 (left) and 2011 (right) show the effects of gold mining in the Peruvian Amazon. The lighter areas show how approximately 20 square miles (50 square km) of forest were cleared by the actions of miners during this time.

GANGS OF MINERS TURNED UP IN THE 1990S. They used highly toxic mercury to flush out the gold. Today, about 193 square miles (500 square km) of rain forest and river have been devastated.

"Water is critical for sustainable development... and the alleviation of poverty and hunger."
United Nations

THE MERCURY POISONED THE FISH that local people ate. It contaminated the river, the air and the soil. The toxic water poisoned the people.

THE MINERS WERE JUST PART OF A MUCH BIGGER PICTURE across the region. Ranchers cleared and burned forest in Brazil, and were ready to kill indigenous people or campaigners who got in their way.

IT WAS THE MINERS WHO POISONED THE RIVERS IN PERU. But they were desperately poor, and could not afford to decontaminate the region when their work was done.

# FARMING AND CROPS

Water is vital for growing the food that we need to stay alive. Some crops are watered naturally, by rainfall, flooding or a wetland habitat. Others need watering by channels, sprays or pipes. Some crops are very 'thirsty,' especially wheat, sugarcane and cotton. Some types of rice need to grow in deep flooded fields, others in shallow fields or irrigated terraces.

## IRRIGATION PROBLEMS

Irrigation can be wasteful as water evaporates and pipes may leak. Too much irrigation makes the water table rise. This sometimes dissolves salty minerals in the soil, which then form a crust on the surface. Too much water extraction for irrigation can also lead to disaster. The Aral Sea, once the fourth largest lake in the world, almost disappeared when water was taken to irrigate cotton fields in Central Asia. That may have been good for farmers, but was terrible news for fishers and lakeside communities, who found themselves living in a desert.

### WATER IN THE DESERT

Artificial irrigation systems have turned normally arid regions, such as parts of California (left), into fertile farmland, but they require a lot of water.

## THIRSTY PRODUCE

Cows and other farm animals need a lot of water to drink and to water the food crops they eat as well.

## NUMBER CRUNCH

Farmers use about 69 percent of all the accessible fresh water in the world.

Abandoned fishing vessels lie beached far from the receding waters of the Aral Sea.

## LET'S DISCUSS...
## FARM ANIMALS

• number about 20 billion worldwide.

• need water and fodder grown as crops.

• provide us with food, wool and other produce.

• take about 1,800 gallons (6,800 L) of water to produce 1 pound (0.5 kg) of beef.

• provide less value for money than cereal or vegetable crops.

• use pasture that could be used to grow crops.

# CITIES AND INDUSTRIES

About 8 percent of fresh water is used in towns and cities, for housing, offices, restaurants, public services, sanitation and swimming pools. However, some cities are built in the most unsuitable places, and face a future of severe water shortages.

The city of Las Vegas uses huge amounts of water, sometimes just to entertain, in what is a very dry region.

## WHO GETS THE WATER?

In the USA, the city of Las Vegas uses up to 166 gallons (629 L) of water per person per day. It has a soaring population, but is built in an arid zone. Its main reservoir, Lake Mead on the dammed Colorado River, runs very low.

The city of Adelaide in South Australia depends on the Murray-Darling river system for its water. Water is extracted for many reasons, so in times of drought there is a risk of the city running dry. The question is, who should have priority – the city dwellers, or the farms and vineyards further upstream?

### LOW WATERS
The white band around the banks of Lake Mead shows just how low the waters in the reservoir have sunk as demand increases but rainfall declines.

Not only can paper production use a lot of water, but paper mills can also produce a large amount of water pollution from organic particles and artificial chemicals.

# MILLS AND MINES

About 23 percent of fresh water is swallowed up by industries such as mining, metals, chemicals and petrochemicals. It may be used for cooling, diluting, dissolving, steaming, cleaning or processing. In the computer industry, very pure water is needed for the manufacturing of silicon chips. It is important not to waste water. Drought is bad news for factories as well as for farms.

## LET'S DISCUSS... THE TOURISM INDUSTRY

- attracts people to sunny parts of the world.
- boosts the local economy and provides employment.
- digs new boreholes for water supply.

- uses huge amounts of water often in areas of shortage or drought.
- pollutes and disturbs marine environments.
- contributes to global warming through increased travel.

# 4 HYDROPOWER

Water has been put to work by humans ever since the water wheel was invented over 2,000 years ago. In modern thermoelectric power stations, water is used as steam to drive the turbines, and also as a coolant. In hydroelectric schemes, the force of the water itself drives the turbines that generate the electricity.

The huge Three Gorges Dam in China was opened in 2003. Some people believe that the mass of water it creates has triggered earthquakes in the area.

## DAMS AND TURBINES

Hydroelectric power is the most widely used of the renewable energy sources, providing 16 percent of the world's electricity. It is planned to double the output by 2050, as this process releases no greenhouse gases. Hydroelectric turbines are often housed in big dams and operate when water from the reservoir is released. The Three Gorges Dam on China's Yangtze River contains 32 giant turbines to generate power. This dam also aims to reduce flooding downstream. Massive concrete dams do present problems. The building of the Three Gorges Dam forced 1.3 million people from their homes, flooded important archaeological sites, increased the risk of landslides and damaged the environment.

### SMALL-SCALE POWER

This image shows a small-scale hydroelectric generator used to produce power for a village in northern Vietnam.

# TIDAL AND WAVE POWER

Bridges or coastal barrages may also house turbines that are driven by the daily surges of the tide. All sorts of clever machines and buoys have also been invented called wave-energy converters (WECs). They make use of the motion of the waves to generate electricity. Wave power is not yet widely used, but it shows promise for the future.

## WAVE POWER

The Pelamis Wave Energy Converter is a large, snake-like device that uses the up-and-down motion of sea waves to produce electricity.

LET'S DISCUSS...
## HYDROELECTRIC POWER

• is a sustainable source of power.

• is clean and does not emit greenhouse gases once built.

• can be generated on a large or a small scale.

• often relies on huge dams, which disrupt the environment.

• uses a lot of carbon-intensive concrete in dam construction.

• disrupts other economic uses of the river.

# USING IT WISELY

Planet Earth is a giant machine for recycling water naturally. Because of climate change, pollution and drought, this system is in danger of breaking down. What can we do about this as individuals? We can campaign for clean water or protest against oil spills. But we can also do a lot in our daily lives to avoid wasting water.

## QUESTION IT!
## DO WE USE WATER WISELY IN THE HOME?

MANY BATHROOMS now have efficient showers that use about 2 gallons (7 L) of water per minute instead of 5 gallons (20 L). Better working showers mean fewer $CO_2$ emissions from the boiler and less waste down the drain.

WASHING MACHINES are now fitted with many more settings than before, such as 'economy wash,' which saves a huge amount of water. The same goes with dishwashers. If you wash up in a sink, don't leave the tap running while you rinse, use a plug.

24 billion

## NUMBER CRUNCH

It has been estimated that, in the US, water equivalent to 24 billion baths is wasted annually because of leaking pipes in homes.

GETTING A HALF-FLUSH OPTION FOR YOUR TOILET OR reducing the full flush could save your family nearly 16,000 gallons (60,000 L) of water during a year.

THE LATEST SHOWERS, washing machines and dishwashers are expensive to buy. Many people have old models that are not as efficient.

# WATER USE IN THE HOME
These figures show how water is used in the average home of a wealthy country.

12.2% washing hands

21.8% flushing toilet

11.7% washing clothes

11.4% other

8.3% washing dishes

5.6% gardening

3.6% cooking and drinking

25.4% bath and shower

WATER IS ALL TOO EASY TO WASTE, AND WE ALL DO IT sometimes. We may use the dishwasher when it is only half-loaded, or boil a full pot of water when we only need one that's half full, or take a bath instead of a shower.

# WHO OWNS WATER?

The question of who owns water has been important throughout history. It is a key issue in dry lands, where water may be a question of survival. Thirst may drive people to conflict, but it may also force them to cooperate and share.

## WATER LAWS

As far as the law in many countries is concerned, the people who own the land around the water are often considered the owners. They have what are called 'riparian' ('river bank') rights and can therefore access and use the water. In other places, the community or the state owns the water and issues permits to those who are entitled to access or use the water.

> In some parts of the world, ownership of the land bordering a river gives you ownership of the river itself.

### WATER PROTEST
In 2005, in the Bolivian city of El Alto, local residents protested against the foreign companies that owned their water supplier.

# PRIVATE OR PUBLIC?

The supply of water may be run as a public service or by a private company. Private supply has often been challenged in less-developed countries. The companies say they are helping ordinary people gain access to a good water system. Protesters say the companies are making a profit from supplying people with what they need simply to stay alive. They say water should not be seen as a commodity like oil or timber. In Bolivia, the privatization of water led to an increase in poverty. As a result, there were popular uprisings and protests, which led to water being returned to public ownership.

LET'S DISCUSS...
PRIVATE WATER COMPANIES

- often claim to be better priced than the government.
- may think more long term than some governments.
- have specialist experience in many countries.

- have a powerful monopoly of supply and no competition.
- tend to put profits before people.
- may have conflicting commercial interests.

# WATER IS A HUMAN RIGHT

Remember that in some parts of the world, clean, safe water is just not available – even out of a tap. Supplying water to all those who are in dire need should be a global priority, as should avoiding waste. Defining water access as an essential right makes that very clear.

## QUESTION IT!
## SHOULD WATER BE TREATED LIKE ANY OTHER COMMODITY?

IN 2010, THE UN DEFINED THE RIGHT TO water as the right of everyone to sufficient, safe, acceptable and physically accessible and affordable water for personal and domestic uses.

AS WITH OXYGEN, WATER is something we all need in order to stay alive, to remain healthy and to prosper. For all these reasons, the right to water has to be seen as an important and universal human right.

### WATER RIGHTS
This poster was created by a European organization that campaigns for worldwide clean drinking water and sanitation.

WATER is a Human Right

"The human right to water is indispensable for leading a life in human dignity. It is a prerequisite for the realization of other human rights."

United Nations resolution, 2010

A UNIVERSAL HUMAN RIGHT IS ONE OF THE BASIC NEEDS that everybody in the world requires in order to live a decent life.

DOESN'T IT MAKE SENSE TO TREAT WATER like any other commodity that can be bought and sold, rather than as a human right?

IF WATER IS NOT JUST A COMMODITY, why did Americans buy 1.7 billion half-liter plastic bottles of water every week in 2015, instead of turning on the tap?

# THE FUTURE OF WATER

In the year 1800, the world was inhabited by about one billion people. Two hundred years later the world population had reached six billion. Today it is 7.5 billion and rising. Ten billion is predicted by 2083. The population clock is racing forward at the same time as the climate change clock. It is a dangerous combination.

The cramped tower blocks of the city of Hong Kong show how human population pressures can dramatically increase the demand for water in a small area.

## PEOPLE ON THE MOVE

Another process already under way is urbanization. For many years, people around the world have been moving from the countryside into the towns and cities. At the same time in Asia and North Africa, war, natural disasters and poverty are forcing people to flee from their homes as refugees.

# THINK WATER

Right now water has to be placed at the center of our planning for the future. It affects both global and local economies, our cities, public health and the environment. We need to plan for water shortages, floods and rising sea levels, because if we do not manage water, it will manage us. If we can save water, however, we can save ourselves.

## NUMBER CRUNCH

In 1800, the planet's population numbered one billion. This has soared to 7.5 billion today and is predicted to be ten billion by 2083.

1800    2016    2083

45

# GLOSSARY

## AQUIFER
Rock, gravel or sand that soak up or trap rainwater.

## ARID ZONE
A region, like the desert around Las Vegas, where the climate is dry and there is very little fresh water available.

## ATMOSPHERE
The air in any particular place or the gases surrounding Earth.

## ATOM
The smallest particle of a chemical element that can exist.

## BACTERIA
A large group of microorganisms, some of which can cause disease and, if found in water, can make people sick.

## BASIN
An area of land that drains into a river or a container that holds water.

## BRACKISH WATER
Also known as briny water, brackish water contains more salt than fresh water but not as much as seawater.

## BRINE
Water that contains high levels of salt.

## CARBON EMISSIONS
The release of carbon dioxide into the atmosphere. Human activities, such as burning oil, coal and gas and cutting down forests, have led to increased levels of carbon dioxide in the atmosphere.

## CISTERN
A waterproof container that holds water, often used to collect rainwater.

## CLIMATE
The weather conditions in an area over a long period.

## COMMODITY
Something that can be bought or sold.

## CONTAMINANT
A substance that pollutes water, making it unsuitable for use or for drinking.

## DESALINATION
The removal of salt from water. Various industrial processes are used to remove salt from seawater.

## DROUGHT
A period of below-average rain that leads to a shortage of water. It can last for days, months or even years.

## DUST BOWL
An area of land where vegetation has been lost and soil reduced to dust, especially as a result of drought or unsuitable farming practices.

## EVAPORATE
Turn from liquid into a vapor.

## FINITE
Having a limit or an end. Water is finite because there is only so much available.

## FOOD CHAIN
A series of plants and animals that are linked because each consumes the one below it in the chain.

## FRESH WATER
Naturally occurring water, such as that found in glaciers, rivers and lakes, that is not salty and is not seawater.

## GREENHOUSE GASES
Gases in the air that trap energy from the Sun and warm the Earth's surface and air. The most common greenhouse gases are water vapor, carbon dioxide and methane.

## HYDROELECTRICITY
The generation of electricity by flowing water, the force of which drives a turbine.

## ICE AGE
A time in the past when temperatures were very cold and glaciers covered large parts of the world.

## INDIGENOUS
Naturally existing in a place or country rather than arriving from another place.

## INTENSIVE FARMING
A way of farming and producing large amounts of crops by using chemicals and machines.

## IRRIGATION
The supply of water to land so that crops and plants can grow.

## MICROBE
A very small living thing, especially one that causes disease, that can only be seen with a microscope.

## NUTRIENTS
Any substance that plants or animals need to live and grow. Drinking water helps to carry nutrients from food to body cells.

## PETROCHEMICAL
Any chemical substance obtained from petroleum or natural gas.

## PRECIPITATION
Water that falls from clouds as rain or in frozen form, such as hail, snow or sleet.

## RENEWABLE ENERGY
Energy that is produced from ongoing sustainable resources, like wind, water or sunlight, rather than finite sources, such as oil or coal.

## RESERVOIR
A large natural or man-made lake used as a source for water.

## RIPARIAN
Relating to the banks of a river. People who own land around water and have riparian rights have the right to use and access the water.

## SANITATION
Conditions essential for public health, especially the provision of clean drinking water and adequate sewage disposal.

## SATURATED
Holding as much water or moisture as can be absorbed.

## SEWER
An underground channel or pipe that carries away drainage water or waste material.

## SUSTAINABLE
Able to be supplied and maintained at a certain level. Water supply needs to be sustainable.

## THERMOELECTRIC
Producing electricity using different temperatures. In modern thermoelectric power stations water is used as steam to drive the turbines and also used as a coolant.

## TUNDRA
A vast, flat, treeless Arctic region where the subsoil is permanently frozen.

## TURBINE
A machine for producing continuous power in which a wheel or rotor is made to revolve often by a fast-moving flow of water.

## UNITED NATIONS (UN)
An association of countries from around the world set up to prevent war and promote international cooperation.

## URBANIZATION
A population shift from rural to urban areas.

## WATER BUTT
A large barrel or tank used for catching and storing rainwater.

## WATER TABLE
The level to which the ground is saturated with water.

## WATER VAPOR
Water in gas form that is produced by evaporation or when water is heated.

# INDEX

## PICTURE CREDITS

The publisher would like to thank the following for their kind permission to reproduce their photographs:
Cover: Nadeem Zulfiqar/Dreamstime.com, Vladislav Gajic/Dreamstime.com; 2–3 Diianadimitrova/Dreamstime.com, 3b Gemenacom/Dreamstime.com, 3t Oleksandr Sokolenko/Dreamstime.com, 3c Welcomia/Dreamstime.com, 3b Photographerlondon/Dreamstime.com; 4 Whitthayap/Dreamstime.com; 5c Sjors737/Dreamstime.com, 5tr Samrat35/Dreamstime.com, 5b Compuinfoto/Dreamstime.com; 6–7 Roman Shyshak/Dreamstime.com; 8 Erectus/Dreamstime.com; 10–11 Jensphotos/Dreamstime.com, 11tr Gemenacom/Dreamstime.com; 12 Tr3gi/Dreamstime.com, 13 Samrat35/Dreamstime.com; 14–15 Irabel8/Dreamstime.com, 14b Asafta/Dreamstime.com; 16–17 Sjors737/Dreamstime.com, 19 Beijing Hetuchuangyi/Dreamstime.com; 20–21 Diianadimitrova/Dreamstime.com, 20b NASA, 21t Patrice Correia/Dreamstime.com, 21cr NASA; 22–23 Chase Dekker/Dreamstime.com, 23 Compuinfoto/Dreamstime.com; 26 Edwardje/Dreamstime.com, 27 Rainer Klotz/Dreamstime.com; 28 Oleksandr Sokolenko/Dreamstime.com, 29t Lighttouch/Dreamstime.com; 30bl NASA, 30br NASA, 31 NASA, 32–33 Vladimir Borodin/Dreamstime.com, 32 b Welcomia/Dreamstime.com, 33t Tulipmix/Dreamstime.com; 34c Kobby Dagan/Dreamstime.com, 34b Shawn Hempel/Dreamstime.com, 35 Moreno Soppelsa/Dreamstime.com, 36–37 Aschwin Prein/Dreamstime.com; 38–39 Alan Crosthwaite/Dreamstime.com; 40b Alamy.com, 41 Pikoli/Dreamstime.com; 42–43 Photographerlondon/Dreamstime.com; 44–45 Imkenneth/Dreamstime.com